CONFIDENCE

Reclaim Your Power,
One Step at a Time

AJI R. MICHAEL

Confidence: Reclaim Your Power, One Step at a Time

Copyright Aji R. Michael, 2025.

Book design: Aji R. Michael

Published by Redefining Living (redefiningliving.org)

Redefining Living books may be purchased for educational, business, or sales promotional use. For information, please email: hello@redefiningliving.org

ISBN: 978-1-8383923-8-3

All rights reserved.

No portion of this book may be reproduced, distributed, or transmitted in any form or by any means without the author's prior written permission. This book offers any Internet addresses (websites, quotes, blogs, etc.) as a resource. They are not intended in any way to be or imply an endorsement by Redefining Living, nor does Redefining Living vouch for the content of these sites for the life of this book.

Contents

Introduction 1
Words to inspire you 4
Chapter 1 6
The Myth of Confidence 6
Chapter 2 16
The Silent Killers of Confidence 16
Chapter 3 34
The Core of Confidence 34
Chapter 4 48
The Link Between Confidence and Power 48
Chapter 5 62
The Framework: Reclaiming Your Confidence (ACE) 62
Chapter 6 75
Your Confidence in Action 75
Appendix 1 81
Coaching Questions and Techniques for ACE 81
Appendix 2 89
Self-Assessment: Rate Your ACE Level 89
References & Notes 95
Other Books By The Author 99
About The Author 100

Aknowledgements..101

Introduction

People call me "Aji", but my full name is Ajibola. It's a name with deep roots in my Nigerian heritage from the western part of the country. Ajibola means "one who wakes up to meet honour, nobility, or wealth." It's a name that reflects gratitude for the blessings and answered prayers my parents received during my conception. They saw it as a sign that I was destined for greatness. And so, they named me Ajibola.

Funny enough, this is typically a male name. But from the very beginning, my mum had a different idea. She called me "Ayinke" — a Yoruba eulogy meaning "one who is praised and pampered." And yes, I was pampered. I was the golden child. From the very first days of my life, I was told I was destined for something special.

Throughout my childhood, I stood out. I became head girl in primary school, one of the best students in my state, and even earned the privilege of being interviewed on national television with my parents. Things fell into place effortlessly. After completing university, I didn't struggle to find a job. I had a thriving fashion and salon business alongside my 9-5 job, living what seemed like an ideal life.

A few years later, everything changed. I was working as a performance manager for the National Health Service in the UK. There was a crisis, and all the managers were called for a briefing. Without warning, my name was mentioned, and I was asked to give an update. Suddenly, I was overwhelmed. My hands shook, my voice faltered, and I couldn't seem to form a sentence. I didn't understand what was happening to me.

A colleague who knew the projects I was working on came to my rescue and gave an excuse on my behalf. But inside, something was shifting.

After the meeting, Christine, a senior manager, called me into a private room. She asked what was going on. She had noticed that I was behaving differently and pointed out my recent silence and the tension in my body language. She gently asked if everything was okay in my marriage. I quickly brushed her off and became defensive, not knowing how to open up. I avoided Christine after that conversation, and our professional relationship never developed further.

Little did I know, my confidence was slipping slowly, imperceptibly, until it had vanished. It wasn't just work; it was my marriage. I was living in a manipulative, abusive, and loveless relationship. I feared being alone more than I feared the emotional pain I was enduring. The effect rippled into every area of my life. I tolerated toxic friendships, constantly trying to please others at my expense. I was afraid of being authentic, of speaking my truth. I hid behind my faith, thinking that perseverance was my only option, but I misunderstood the concept of endurance. I didn't know how to set healthy boundaries or how to balance humility with self-respect.

On the outside, everything seemed perfect. I had a good job, a family, a nice home. But inside, I was struggling. I was fighting a battle for my soul, trying to reclaim the woman I once was — Ajibola, the one destined for greatness, and Ayinke, who was meant to be celebrated and loved. I was lost in the conflict between who I was expected to be and who I truly was.

It took years of emotional turmoil, years of therapy and coaching before I could begin to reclaim my power and confidence. It wasn't easy. I had to learn to trust myself again.

Confidence, for anyone who has been through trauma, is not something that can be easily restored. It's not a straight path. The effects of trauma leave a lasting mark on you, and every time you think you're about to soar, that scar can pull you back down.

But here's the truth I want you to hear: Your confidence has not been destroyed. It's been buried under layers of pain, self-doubt, and fear. But it's still there, waiting to be reclaimed.

This book is here to help you reclaim what's rightfully yours: your confidence, your power, and your peace of mind. I know firsthand how hard it can be to rebuild after life has dealt you some tough blows. But I also know that it's possible. Through the stories, tools, and steps I'll share in this book, I want to show you how to regain control and reclaim your confidence — one step at a time.

I'm not here to tell you that it will be easy, but I am here to tell you that it is absolutely worth it. No matter where you've been or what's happened to you, reclaiming your confidence is a possibility—it's your birthright.

WORDS TO INSPIRE YOU

This book echoes a recent discussion my spouse and I had about the importance of nurturing our children's confidence and how our actions as parents profoundly shape their future. It reassures me that we are moving in the right direction.

While the book is primarily written for women, its message has universal appeal. The lessons resonate far beyond their intended audience, as living authentically and confronting our fears are challenges that transcend gender.

The real-life experiences shared in the book are particularly compelling. Stories of women who allowed societal perceptions to define them, those who recognised the path to trouble and quickly reclaimed their true selves, and those who now "ACE" their confidence illustrate the diverse nature of life's journey. Some inspire vulnerability, courage, and honesty, while others reflect non-acceptance and possible stagnation. These narratives offered me a gentle mirror to reflect on where I stand in my own journey.

I invite parents to prioritise reading this book as it allows them to redefine their lives and create an environment that fosters authenticity. By committing to mindful actions, they can shape a future for their children rooted in confidence and self-awareness, leaving a lasting, positive impact.

As I reflect further on the content of this book, I am struck by its central message, particularly for women: the new order is authenticity. You don't have to pretend to be strong all the time or give the impression that your life is perfectly in order. Vulnerability, far from being a weakness, is a profound strength.

The book's honesty was striking. It emphasises that lying to oneself only robs you of the power to walk confidently and authentically. It urges us to seek genuine love—not the kind purchased with money or gained through the pretence of being someone we are not to fit into a particular class or group. Instead, it challenges us to be strong, courageous, and intentional about our lives. Take charge of your journey: seek counsel, pursue therapy if needed, and reassess your social circle—changing it if the people around you no longer support your growth.

Here is my final resolve: intellectuality and wisdom exist on two distinct spectrums. It is the latter—wisdom—that we should seek and apply to live a truly authentic and fulfilling life.

Feyikemi Oyewole
Life Transformation and Youth Leadership Coach

CHAPTER 1

The Myth of Confidence

1.1 Common Misconceptions About Confidence

We've all seen it. The polished image of someone with boundless confidence — the person who seems to have it all together, effortlessly succeeding in every area of their life. Society tells us that confidence looks a certain way. It's the flashy suit, the bold social media posts, the high-powered job, the perfectly curated Instagram life. As we've been taught, confidence is about exuding power, showing off, and being unshakable. But what if I told you that this image of confidence — the one we often try to live up to — is a myth?

You see, I grew up with the idea that confidence was a shiny, external thing—something you could see in the perfectly styled photos, the job promotions, the designer clothes, and the people who seemed to walk into a room like they owned it. And for a long time, I bought into that myth. I believed that to be confident, I needed to check all those boxes—success, wealth, a perfect image—I needed to fit into that picture-perfect mould.

But here's the truth I've learned the hard way: Confidence is not about showing off, being loud, or having the world's approval. Confidence isn't about being perfect. In fact, it's the opposite. Real confidence is about being raw, authentic, and vulnerable. It's about embracing who you are, flaws and all, and owning every part of yourself — not just the polished parts but also the messy, broken, uncertain parts.

I know what it's like to live in a world that tells you that confidence means being flawless. I've been there. There was a time when I thought I wasn't confident unless I could show the world an image of success. I had a career I was proud of, a family, a business, and yet, something inside me was broken. I was living in a loveless, toxic marriage, surrounded by people who didn't truly see me. I put on a mask, convinced that being "fine" on the outside would mean I was fine on the inside too. But deep down, I knew the truth. I was anything but fine.

I couldn't understand why, with everything going "right" on the surface, I still felt like I was slowly losing myself. It wasn't until much later that I realised that the world's idea of confidence isn't the same as true confidence. True confidence isn't about perfection; it's about permission to be yourself in all your mess and glory. True confidence comes from within and doesn't need to prove itself to anyone. It just is.

You don't need to be a high-flyer or wear the latest designer clothes to feel confident. You don't need to have all your life's ducks in a row or show up with a shiny facade to be worthy of confidence. Confidence isn't about the job title, the fancy car, or the perfectly curated Instagram post. Confidence is about accepting yourself in the moment — as you are — without needing external validation. It's about being comfortable with your imperfections and learning to stand in your truth, even when it feels scary.

And here's the thing: That's what makes it so difficult for many of us. We've been conditioned to believe that confidence must be loud, brash, or external. But real confidence, the kind that lasts is quieter. It's the kind of confidence that comes when you're at peace with who you are when you no longer need to put on a performance for the world. It's raw. It's vulnerable. It's the courage to show up as your true self — unpolished, imperfect, and real.

In this chapter, I want to shatter the myth that confidence is external and unattainable. I want to remind you that confidence doesn't come from outside of you; it comes from within. You can have a thriving career and a successful business and still struggle with self-doubt. You can have the world's applause and feel you're not enough. But that doesn't mean you're not worthy of true confidence. It simply means you've been taught to look for it in the wrong places.

So, let's begin the journey of reclaiming your confidence — not the fake, superficial version, but the kind that allows you to stand tall in your own skin, even when life isn't perfect. Let's start by letting go of the myths and embracing confidence: the quiet strength to be yourself, no matter what the world tells you it should look like. Confidence is not a destination; it's a practice. And it starts with loving yourself, flaws and all.

1.2 Women Who Have Battled the Confidence Myth

When I think about the women I've met over the years — women whose lives looked perfect on the outside — I am struck by the contrast between their outward strength and the hidden battles they were fighting. It's easy to assume that someone with a strong exterior must have it all together. But repeatedly, I've been reminded that confidence isn't about the facade. It's about what's happening on the inside.

Clara – The Church Leader

I first met Clara at church. She was one of the women who always seemed to have everything together—always there with a smile, ready to serve, and the first to step in when needed. She was the kind of woman you couldn't help but admire—calm, graceful, and composed. She had this quiet authority about her that made people trust her without question. Over time, I've developed a friendship with Clara and often shared food recipes.

One day, during a women's group retreat, she pulled me aside, her voice shaky as she shared something that completely surprised me.

"I'm terrified," Clara admitted, her eyes filled with tears. "I feel like I'm drowning in expectations — my family's, the church's, even my own. I'm expected to be the strong one, the one who always has everything under control. But what if I'm just pretending? What if they knew how broken I really am?"

I was stunned. Clara, the woman who held everything together for everyone else, was crumbling on the inside. She talked about feeling like an imposter in her own life, afraid that one day someone would expose her as someone who wasn't as confident as they thought. Behind the calm, composed woman I had admired was a woman who felt weak, unworthy, and unsure of herself. She had built her life around being "the strong one, " yet deep down, she was struggling to believe in her own strength.

Clara had fallen victim to the myth of confidence — the belief that to be confident, you must always be in control, never vulnerable. But in reality, her true strength would come when she embraced her imperfections and stopped pretending she was invincible.

Megan – The Colleague Who Had It All

Megan was a colleague I met in my professional career. She was sharp, assertive, and always on top of her game. When she entered a room, heads turned. She was the kind of woman who inspired respect. Megan had a corner office, a successful career, and a well-curated life. She had every reason to feel confident — and, in many ways, she did. But when we worked together on a project, something shifted in our interactions.

Late one afternoon, Megan opened up to me as we finalised a presentation. "I'm exhausted," she said, her voice small for the first time I'd ever heard. "It feels like no matter how much I achieve, it's never enough. I'm always proving myself — to my team, family, and friends. It's like I can't take a break. What if they all find out I'm not as good as they think I am?"

I could hardly believe what I was hearing. Megan, the confident, accomplished woman everyone looked up to, constantly feared being exposed as a fraud. She worked harder than anyone I knew, not because she loved her job, but because she was terrified of failing, of showing any sign of weakness. She believed that if she weren't constantly perfect, people would stop respecting her.

Megan's story broke my heart because I realised that she, too, had bought into the myth that confidence meant never showing any cracks or revealing vulnerability. She was so caught up in the idea that she needed to be flawless to be worthy of respect that she couldn't even allow herself to rest.

Tasha – The Neighbourhood Beauty

Tasha was a woman I knew from my neighbourhood. She had a beauty that turned heads—the kind that made you do a double-take. Her long, shiny hair, perfect skin, and effortless elegance made her the envy of many. She was the woman everyone assumed had it all—from the outside, at least. But one day, we sat down for a cup of coffee, and she told me a story that shattered the image I had of her.

"You know," Tasha began, nervously stirring her coffee, "people think I've got it all together because of how I look. But that's the thing — it's just a mask. I feel like I'm constantly judged for my appearance and hate it. Sometimes, I think that the only thing people see is my beauty. But what if they knew that inside? I was terrified. Terrified that no one will ever really see me, the real me. What if I'm just a pretty face with no substance?"

Tasha went on to share how her whole life had been reduced to her looks. She had been complimented for her beauty, but deep down, she wondered if anyone truly saw her. She felt invisible, not because of her appearance but because she couldn't break free from the expectations attached to it. She often felt that people didn't respect her for who she truly was, only for what they could see.

Tasha's story resonated with me deeply. She had internalised the myth that beauty was enough to command respect and confidence, but the truth was far from it. Confidence, she learned the hard way, isn't about what others see on the surface. It's about who you are on the inside — and learning to believe you are worthy of respect, regardless of your appearance.

These women — Clara, Megan, and Tasha — all lived with the weight of the myth of confidence. Their stories may seem different on the surface, but they share a common thread: the belief that confidence can be measured by external accomplishments, appearance, or control. But each of them — just like you — had to realise that true confidence isn't something that can be seen or measured. It's felt on the inside and built on authenticity, vulnerability, and the courage to be yourself, flaws and all.

1.3 Debunking the Confidence Myth

For much of my life, I believed that confidence was something you either had or didn't have. It was like a shiny, unattainable prize that only certain people possessed. I thought it was about perfection — always looking good, always being on top of your game, never showing vulnerability. I saw confidence as something external, something to be worn like a badge of honour. I believed that those who exuded confidence had it all together, and I was left feeling like I was always a step behind, constantly striving but never quite measuring up.

I remember a time in my early adulthood when I was brimming with ambition but crippled by self-doubt. I had the career, the business, and even the image that looked perfect on the outside. But inside, I felt like a fraud. There was always a voice inside me telling me I wasn't good enough, that I couldn't trust myself, that I wasn't worthy of the success I had. So, I worked harder and tried to achieve more, thinking that if I could just be perfect, I would finally feel confident.

But the truth is, perfection was never the answer. It was an illusion that trapped me in a cycle of self-criticism and external validation.

When I look back now, I can trace this deep-rooted belief about myself all the way back to my childhood. I grew up in a household where praise was often reserved for accomplishments. I was a high achiever — a top student, a leader among my peers — and I was frequently told how proud my parents were of my success. But what was never really acknowledged was who I was as a person, apart from my achievements. I began to internalise the idea that my worth was tied to what I could do, not who I truly was.

In my early years, incidents and moments I pushed deep down into my subconscious began shaping my belief about my worth. The constant comparisons to others and the moments of feeling invisible or being overlooked despite my efforts planted seeds of doubt in my young mind. I didn't realise it at the time, but these experiences were chipping away at my confidence in ways I couldn't yet understand.

It wasn't until much later in life, after years of struggle and emotional turmoil, that I began to uncover just how deeply these incidents had impacted me. I was living my life according to a belief system formed not from my own truth but from the expectations and perceptions of others. I was chasing external validation, thinking I would finally feel worthy and confident if I could just meet those expectations.

But when I started working with a coach and later a therapist, I began to peel back the layers of my life. I realised that this underlying belief that I wasn't enough influenced many of the decisions I had made, the relationships I had settled for, and the jobs I had taken. I was unaware of how deeply these wounds had shaped my life choices. They were so deeply buried in my subconscious that I couldn't even recognise them until someone held up a mirror for me.

I had to confront the truth: the way I was living wasn't me. It was me trying to live up to a version of myself that wasn't rooted in who I truly was but in who I thought I was supposed to be. And that, I realised, was not confidence. That was survival. I had been surviving for so long, playing roles, meeting expectations, and trying to be someone I wasn't.

I had been looking for my confidence in all the wrong places — in my achievements, in the approval of others, in how I looked on the outside. But none of that could give me the peace and the strength I craved.

True confidence, I came to understand, isn't about perfection. It isn't about having everything figured out or wearing a perfect mask. It's about being raw and vulnerable enough to admit that you are enough just as you are — no achievements, no external validation required. Confidence is about knowing that you are worthy of love and respect, not because of what you do or look, but because of who you are.

When I began to unravel these layers and reconnect with my true self, I discovered that confidence was never unattainable. It wasn't reserved for other people. It was always within me, hidden beneath the layers of doubt and fear. The more I embraced my authentic self, imperfections and all, the more

I started to feel my confidence grow. I stopped needing external validation to feel worthy. I began to trust myself, to trust that my worth wasn't contingent on my success, failures, appearances, or accomplishments.

And you know what? I began to feel a freedom I had never known before. A freedom that came from within. A freedom that didn't depend on what anyone else thought of me. This was the real confidence I had been searching for all along — the kind that is grounded in self-acceptance, authenticity, and the courage to show up as you are.

I share this with you because I know what it feels like to think confidence is something you'll never have, something only the "lucky" or the "perfect" people can attain. But let me tell you: confidence isn't a distant dream. It's a practice, a choice, and it starts with you — with the decision to stop chasing perfection and start embracing the beautiful, messy, authentic person you are.

CHAPTER 2

The Silent Killers of Confidence

2.1 The Impact of Abusive Relationships, Toxic Workplaces, and Trauma

When we talk about confidence, we often think of it as a trait we either have or don't have, something that comes naturally or is hard to find. But the truth is that confidence is not only a result of our personality or actions — it is deeply affected by our experiences, especially the traumatic ones. These experiences, whether they come from childhood, toxic relationships, or difficult work environments, can be silent killers of our confidence. And the worst part is, sometimes we don't even realise just how deeply these experiences have scarred us until they begin to show up in our lives in subtle, destructive ways.

You see, trauma doesn't just affect your emotional state; it literally rewires your brain. Neuroscientific studies have shown that traumatic experiences — like an abusive relationship, a toxic workplace, or childhood neglect — leave a lasting imprint on the brain, altering how we think, behave, and perceive ourselves. When we go through trauma, our brain enters survival mode. The amygdala, the part of the brain responsible for processing emotions, becomes hyperactive, while the prefrontal cortex, the area that governs reasoning and decision-making, becomes less effective.

This means that in the wake of trauma, our ability to make confident decisions and trust ourselves is significantly impaired.

In a toxic environment, whether it's a controlling relationship or a workplace that constantly undermines you, your confidence is slowly eroded. You begin to doubt your worth, abilities, and instincts. And it's not just a fleeting feeling. Over time, repeated exposure to these environments — where you're constantly invalidated, belittled, or made to feel small — wears you down to the point where you begin to believe the negative things people say about you.

When I went through my own difficult relationship, I didn't realise at the time how much my confidence was being chipped away, piece by piece. I was so wrapped up in trying to survive the emotional and psychological abuse that I never stopped to consider how it was changing the way I saw myself. Every harsh word, every control tactic, every moment of neglect left an imprint. Over time, I became less and less sure of who I was and more and more afraid of being alone, unloved, and judged. I doubted myself constantly, unsure if I was making the right decisions. My self-worth became attached to others thought of me — particularly my spouse. I started to believe I wasn't good enough if I didn't meet certain expectations.

This experience wasn't unique to me. Toxic environments, especially those where we're constantly criticised or controlled, can cause a similar pattern of damage to confidence. Psychology has long shown that being surrounded by criticism from a partner, boss, or even family member affects our ability to see ourselves clearly. In these environments, we don't just face external rejection; we internalise it, turning it into self-rejection. We start to believe that something is wrong with us. This type of thinking leads to a self-fulfilling prophecy: we begin to make decisions based on our fear of rejection instead of our inner truth.

It's not just intimate relationships that cause this kind of damage. Toxic workplaces can have a similar effect. A colleague once told me how she felt invisible in her work environment. She was a highly capable woman, but in her company, she was constantly overlooked, her ideas dismissed, and her contributions ignored. Over time, she began to believe that her opinions didn't matter and that she wasn't good enough to make an impact. She'd worked her way up to a leadership position, but the constant undermining from her peers had eroded her self-belief. She no longer trusted her judgment, and her confidence had crumbled, even though she was still successful on the outside.

In many ways, trauma and toxic environments function like an emotional disease. It's insidious. It seeps in slowly and subtly, often without you even realising it. It changes the way you think about yourself, how you see your worth, and how you make decisions. And it's not just emotional scars. Studies in neuroscience reveal that trauma affects how our brain processes information. The more we experience stress and trauma, the more our brain becomes wired for fear and survival. This can lead to heightened anxiety, self-doubt, and a constant state of hypervigilance — where we're always on guard, never quite at peace with who we are or what we're doing.

This is particularly evident in childhood trauma. I was surprised when I began to work with my therapist and coach how much my early experiences had influenced my sense of self-worth. As a child, I learned to hide my emotions and put on a brave face because that was the only way to get through certain situations. But those behaviours, while they may have served me at the time, eventually turned into patterns of self-suppression. I didn't know it then, but I had learned not to trust myself. I had learned to ignore my needs and voice and to listen to what others told me I should do, feel, or believe. These deep-seated beliefs about my worth were not even conscious at first. They were buried so deeply in my subconscious that they didn't surface until years later, when I started to unpack the trauma with a coach and therapist.

The same is true for so many others who experience toxic environments or traumatic events. The pain is stored in the body, our thoughts, and how we see the world. When you've been told for so long that you're not enough and subjected to constant criticism or emotional manipulation, it's no surprise that your confidence becomes fragile. You've been conditioned to doubt yourself.

But here's the good news: Reclaiming your confidence is never too late. Yes, trauma and toxic environments can leave deep scars, but those scars don't have to define who you are or your future. Neuroscience tells us that the brain is neuroplastic — meaning it has the ability to change and adapt. With the right tools and support, you can rewire your brain, heal from the wounds, and start rebuilding your confidence. You can heal from the past and rebuild a sense of self-worth that's rooted in who you truly are — not in what others have told you or in the trauma you've experienced.

I know this because I've lived it. It wasn't easy, but through therapy, coaching, and deep self-reflection, I started to break free from the toxic beliefs I had carried with me for so long. I began to trust myself again. I stopped believing the lies I had been told. And little by little, I began to feel my confidence return, stronger than ever.

If you're reading this and you can relate to any part of my story — whether it's from a toxic relationship, a difficult childhood, or a toxic workplace — I want you to know that you can rebuild your confidence, too. It's not about perfection. It's about healing, uncovering your true worth, and trusting that you are enough, just as you are. The first step is recognising that your confidence was never truly lost — it's always been inside of you, waiting to be reclaimed. And with each step you take towards healing, it will grow stronger.

2.2 How Trauma Erodes Self-Belief

When we experience trauma, it doesn't always look like what we see in the movies or hear about in dramatic stories. Trauma can often be quiet and sneaky, like a thief in the night, taking bits and pieces of who we are without us even realising. Over time, it chips away at our self-belief, often in ways that are so subtle we don't even recognise it until we've lost our footing and wonder how we got here.

Looking back, I can see just how much my own experiences with trauma eroded my confidence, piece by piece. But at the time, I didn't know what was happening. I thought I was simply "getting through" life, doing what I had to do to survive. Little did I know, I was allowing my trauma to quietly control my decisions, my beliefs, and my perception of myself.

Aji R. Michael

The Breakdown of My Self-Worth

One of the most powerful experiences I had was in my marriage. I had always prided myself on being strong, independent, and capable. But living in an emotionally and psychologically abusive marriage slowly began to chip away at my sense of self. It was a slow erosion. It wasn't just one big event that shattered me — it was the constant manipulation, the subtle undermining, and the dismissive comments that started to feel like they were echoing in my head long after they were made.

At first, I didn't notice how much it was affecting me. I kept telling myself that it was just the stress of life, that it was normal to have disagreements, and that this was just part of being married. But as time went on, I started to feel smaller and smaller. I doubted myself constantly, second-guessed my decisions and feared expressing my thoughts or feelings. What if he didn't agree with me? What if I said something wrong? What if I disappointed him?

This whole experience played out during an incident I described in the introductory part of this book. A particular moment when I was asked to speak at a meeting at work — when my confidence should have been at its peak. I was well-respected in my role, with years of experience and expertise. But when I stood up to speak, I froze. My mind went blank. My voice shook. I felt like the whole room could see how inadequate I was. At that moment, all I could hear was the voice of my spouse in my head, telling me I wasn't good enough and that I was just pretending to be confident. The trauma of years of emotional abuse had planted seeds of doubt so deeply in my subconscious that I couldn't access the self-belief I once had.

That moment was a turning point for me. I realised that my lack of confidence wasn't just about the external pressures of work or life. It was deeply tied to the trauma of being in a relationship where I had been made to feel small, insignificant, and unworthy. Over time, I had internalised these messages. The trauma had rewritten the story I told myself about who I was, what I deserved, and what I could achieve.

Childhood Trauma: The Seed of Doubt

Trauma doesn't just happen in adulthood. Sometimes, it starts in childhood, where the seeds of doubt are planted long before we even understand the power of self-belief. I can trace much of my self-doubt back to my early years — to the subtle messages I received as a child about being "good enough." Growing up in a culture where academic success and outward achievement were highly valued, I always felt the pressure to excel. But at home, things weren't always perfect. There were moments when I felt dismissed, invisible, or as though my achievements weren't enough. I remember being praised for good grades but never really feeling celebrated for who I was as a person. It was always about what I could do, never about who I was.

At the time, I didn't realise how much this affected my sense of self-worth. I didn't feel like I was enough, just as I was. I thought I wasn't valuable if I wasn't excelling, achieving, or performing at a high level. That belief followed me throughout my life. I began associating my worth with what I could accomplish, and any failure felt like a personal attack on my value. After years of therapy and self-reflection, it was only later that I understood how much of my confidence had been tied to my accomplishments and how much of my self-belief had been eroded by the unspoken belief that I was only worthy if I was perfect.

Toxic Workplaces: Constant Undermining

Even as an adult, the environment around me eroded my self-belief. I remember a particular job I had early in my career. I was surrounded by colleagues who constantly undermined each other, a toxic work culture that thrived on competition, gossip, and belittling others. I always stepped up, worked hard, and tried to keep things together, but it seemed that no matter what I did, it was never enough.

My ideas were dismissed, my contributions overlooked, and the respect I longed for never seemed to materialise. Ultimately, I was let go from my position due to a minor issue related to childcare responsibilities, claiming that such obligations were incompatible with my role.

Another experience was during a performance review at a director level; I was told that I wasn't "assertive enough" and needed to be "more aggressive" in pushing my ideas. Being the only black female on the board, each day felt like a constant war. It left me confused and frustrated. I had worked hard, but my hard work seemed invisible to everyone around me. No matter how much I gave, I felt I wasn't seen. That sense of invisibility, that lack of recognition, chipped away at my belief in myself. I began to question whether I was good enough to be there. The toxic environment made me feel like I was always one step away from being exposed as a fraud.

As I stepped away from the role yet again, a sense of inevitability washed over me. It wasn't due to a concerted effort to undermine me by others; rather, it was the painful realisation that I had not been authentic—I was merely mirroring their behaviours and attitudes. In that moment, I recognised how disingenuous that was, a betrayal of my true self. A part of me longed for a resource, perhaps a book filled with wisdom, that could have prepared me for this bittersweet reality, guiding me to embrace my individuality during such pivotal times.

The Accumulation of Pain

These experiences — whether in my marriage, childhood, or career — didn't just affect me in isolated moments. They piled up, one on top of the other until I found myself standing in a place where I didn't recognise myself. The quiet whispers of self-doubt, the constant questioning of my worth, the belief that I wasn't enough — they all stemmed from the trauma I had experienced. In a way, these events shaped the lens through which I saw myself and the world.

Trauma doesn't just disappear. It stays with you. It seeps into the way you make decisions, the way you interact with others, and the way you view yourself. But here's the truth I want you to hear: you don't have to stay stuck in these beliefs. You don't have to let trauma define you. I can tell you, from my journey, that healing is possible. It takes time, courage, and confronting the things that hurt — but it is possible.

Trauma can erode your confidence, yes, but it can also be the very thing that leads you to reclaim it. When you recognise how trauma has shaped you, you can begin to heal. And with that healing, your true confidence — the one that doesn't rely on perfection or external validation — can rise. The process is not linear, but every step you take toward healing brings you closer to the confidence you've always had within you.

2.3 Women Who Rebuilt Confidence After Trauma

During my healing journey, I attended a support group that changed my life. At the time, I was separated from my husband, walking through the painful and deeply personal process of reclaiming my sense of self. I was still a church leader, deeply involved in the community, yet I felt the weight of my situation like a secret I could never fully share. My pastor, who was well-meaning, had asked that my separation not be made public, as I held a leadership position. So, I struggled in silence, trying to keep my brokenness hidden behind the walls I'd so carefully built. It was hard to be authentic and feel confident in a place where I didn't feel I could truly speak my truth.

For months, I carried the burden of isolation. On the outside, I was still doing the work, still smiling, still leading, but inside, I felt like I was drowning. My confidence, once strong and unshakeable, had slipped away, and I couldn't find the words or the courage to admit it — to myself, let alone to anyone else. I wasn't sure how to reconcile the woman I was on the outside with the broken one I was on the inside.

But then came the turning point — a moment that would change everything.

During one of our leaders' meetings, something in me snapped. I couldn't keep pretending that everything was fine. I couldn't keep hiding behind my role. I had to speak the truth, no matter how hard it felt or how terrified I was. So, with a shaky voice and a heart full of fear, I shared what was happening in my life. I shared my pain, my shame, my vulnerability. And in that moment, everything shifted. The room fell silent for a moment, and then, one by one, the women who had been sitting there in the same quiet pain began to speak.

Grace's Story

Grace was the first woman to share. I remember her voice trembling as she spoke, but there was a quiet power behind it. She shared that she had been in an abusive marriage for years, one where she had been controlled, belittled, and emotionally torn down until she didn't recognise herself anymore. She told us about when she realised she had to leave and how she felt like she was completely alone in the unknown. But the most striking part of her story was when she said, "I didn't know I had strength until I left. And then I realised my strength was always inside me, just waiting to be uncovered."

Grace's words hit me hard. I was in the middle of my own struggle, questioning whether I had the strength to continue forward. But here she was, a woman who had come out of a marriage that had nearly destroyed her, reclaiming her confidence one day at a time. She was proof that even in the darkest moments, you could rise. She spoke about the therapy and support groups she attended and how, bit by bit, she had built her self-belief back up. She learned to love herself again. It wasn't an easy journey, but it was hers. And she took it. Her story gave me the courage to believe that, one day, I, too, could reclaim my confidence.

Linda's Story

Linda's story was different but equally inspiring. She had spent years in a toxic work environment where her abilities were constantly undermined. She was the "yes woman," always pleasing others and pushing her own needs aside until she had nothing left to give. She shared how, for years, she had been in a toxic cycle — working harder and harder to gain approval, never feeling good enough no matter what she did. Her confidence, once soaring, had slowly eroded until she was barely recognisable to herself.

But Linda's transformation was nothing short of miraculous. She spoke about how she decided that enough was enough after one particularly hurtful incident at work. She left the toxic environment, started her own business, and surrounded herself with people who saw her worth. She said something that stuck with me: "It's not the environment that controls your worth. It's you. You have the power to choose what you will accept and who you will allow in your life." Linda's words reminded us that the circumstances of our lives don't define our value — we get to choose what we allow to shape us.

Maria's Story

Maria's story was one I could deeply relate to because her trauma came from childhood, much like mine. Maria had grown up in an environment where love was conditional, based on her achievements. She was praised when she excelled in school or sports, but there was no love or recognition when she failed. This pattern continued into her adult life, where she became a perfectionist, always chasing the next achievement to feel worthy of love and attention.

What struck me about Maria's story was when she realised that the constant need to prove herself wasn't about the outside world — it was about the belief she had carried from childhood that her worth was tied to what she could achieve. It took her years to understand that her confidence was not something she had to earn through accomplishments. Her confidence was her birthright, buried under a mountain of unrealistic expectations. Maria's journey of healing came when she learned to embrace her flaws, recognise her worth beyond her achievements, and stop trying to earn love and acceptance.

Her story taught me that true confidence doesn't depend on the applause of others. It's about knowing, deep in your soul, that you are worthy simply because you exist.

Listening to these women share their stories was nothing short of transformative for me. Each had faced unimaginable pain, yet each had found a way to rebuild their confidence. They didn't do it by pretending everything was fine or hiding behind perfection. They did it by embracing their vulnerability, doing the work to heal, and accepting the truth that they were worthy of love, respect, and happiness—regardless of what they had been through.

Their stories scared me, yes, but they also gave me hope. They showed me that no matter how broken we feel or how deep the trauma, it's possible to rise again. They inspired me to take the next step in my healing journey, stop hiding behind my role, and start being true to myself.

At that moment, I realised that confidence isn't something we are given by others. It's something we must give ourselves. It is the courage to share our stories, the bravery to heal, and the strength to stand up and say, "I am worthy, just as I am."

Their journeys weren't easy, but they were proof that transformation was possible. And if they could do it, so could I. So could you. And that's the message I want you to take away from this: you are not alone, and your healing is possible. You can rebuild your confidence, no matter what you've been through. And I'm here to walk that journey with you.

2.4 Psychological and Emotional Effects on Confidence

The effects of trauma and toxic environments on our confidence are not just something we feel in the moment. They ripple through our lives, shaping how we view ourselves, interact with others, and navigate the world. The psychological and emotional impacts of these experiences can be profound, often leaving us questioning our worth, abilities, and place in the world.

Scientific research tells us that these experiences do more than just hurt emotionally; they literally reshape the brain and how we process information, making it harder for us to trust ourselves and our instincts. Trauma, whether it's from childhood, a toxic relationship, or an abusive workplace, impacts the core of who we are, and often, we don't realise the damage until it's far along in the process.

The Science Behind Self-Doubt: How Trauma Impacts the Brain

Neuroscience has shown that traumatic experiences can physically alter the structure of our brains. The brain's response to trauma is immediate: when we experience emotional or psychological pain, the amygdala—the part of the brain responsible for processing emotions and reactions—goes into overdrive, while the prefrontal cortex, the area responsible for reasoning, decision-making, and managing social behaviour, becomes less active. Essentially, when we are going through, our emotional brain takes over, while our logical brain struggles to keep up.

This is why, when we experience prolonged emotional stress or trauma, it can feel like we're stuck in a loop of self-doubt and fear. It's as if our brains have been conditioned to perceive threats and danger, making it difficult to trust ourselves or our decisions. When our brain is caught in this cycle, confidence — the ability to trust ourselves and our instincts — becomes harder to achieve.

A study published in Psychiatry Research found that traumatic experiences, particularly those occurring in childhood, can reduce the brain's capacity to regulate emotions, leading to long-term issues with self-esteem and confidence. In these cases, we may find ourselves constantly questioning our worth or doubting our capabilities, even when we have every reason to feel confident.

The Emotional Toll: From Shame to Isolation

On the emotional side, trauma can create a sense of deep shame. When we've been emotionally or physically abused, when we've been belittled, criticised, or rejected, it's easy to internalise the hurt. We begin to believe that something is wrong with us, that we do not deserve love, respect, or happiness. This emotional toll can cause us to shrink away from opportunities or avoid situations where we might have to stand up for ourselves or be vulnerable.

Shame is a powerful emotion that silences us. In fact, research by Dr. Brené Brown, a renowned expert on shame and vulnerability, shows that shame can prevent us from living authentically. It isolates us from others, making us feel like we're not good enough to be seen for who we truly are. When we're caught in the grip of shame, we stop expressing ourselves freely and start hiding the parts of us that we think others won't love or accept. This, of course, erodes our confidence because confidence is built on the foundation of self-acceptance.

The psychological effects of shame can leave us feeling constantly on edge, afraid that we will be exposed for who we really are. It creates an emotional wall between us and the world, forcing us to retreat into ourselves. And in that retreat, our confidence fades.

Self-Doubt: The Subtle Erosion of Confidence

What's often harder to recognise is the subtle nature of self-doubt. It doesn't always show up as an obvious sign of low self-esteem, but it whispers in our minds in the quiet moments when we're making decisions or reflecting on our actions. "Am I good enough?" "Should I even try?" "What if they don't like me?" These thoughts, which might seem harmless at first, slowly chip away at our confidence, leaving us in constant uncertainty.

Psychological studies have shown that self-doubt is a natural reaction to past trauma or negative experiences. A study in the Journal of Traumatic Stress demonstrated that individuals who had experienced childhood abuse or neglect were more likely to struggle with chronic self-doubt and a diminished sense of self-worth well into adulthood. Over time, this internalised self-doubt can begin to feel like a permanent part of who we are, making it difficult to take risks, speak up, or even try new things.

It feeds the idea that we're not capable, that we don't deserve success or happiness.

But what's fascinating — and perhaps the most hopeful part of this — is that our brains are incredibly adaptable. Neuroplasticity, the brain's ability to rewire itself, offers us the chance to heal from the damage caused by trauma. With time, self-compassion, and the right tools, we can begin to change the way we think about ourselves and rebuild the foundation of our confidence.

The Cycle of Emotional and Psychological Impact

The cycle of trauma and its impact on confidence is often self-reinforcing. The more we experience emotional pain, the more it affects how we perceive ourselves, which affects our ability to trust ourselves. For example, when we experience rejection or criticism, we may start to believe that we're simply not good enough. This belief becomes entrenched, leading us to avoid situations where we might be judged or criticised, reinforcing the belief that we're incapable or unworthy. It's a vicious cycle.

Research has shown that this type of cycle can be particularly damaging in intimate relationships or toxic workplaces. A study published in the Journal of Social and Clinical Psychology found that individuals in abusive relationships often experience what's known as "learned helplessness." This is a state in which they believe that no matter what they do, they can't change their circumstances. This learned helplessness chips away at their self-confidence and causes them to stop taking action to improve their lives.

The same cycle can occur in toxic workplaces, where individuals are constantly undermined or belittled. Over time, they begin to doubt their own abilities, avoid taking initiative, and shrink back from opportunities. This diminished self-belief doesn't just affect their professional life; it spills over into their personal lives as well, leaving them feeling unworthy and disconnected.

Rebuilding Confidence: The Road to Recovery

While trauma, abuse, and toxic environments can significantly impact our confidence, the good news is that healing is possible. Psychological studies have proven that when we begin to challenge the negative beliefs that stem from trauma, we can begin to rewire our brains and restore our sense of self-worth. Therapy, coaching, mindfulness, and self-compassion practices have been shown to be incredibly effective in rebuilding confidence. They help us unlearn the limiting beliefs that trauma has ingrained in us, and instead, we start to cultivate a more positive, supportive relationship with ourselves.

The path to recovery is not easy and doesn't happen overnight. But it starts with recognising the impact of trauma and giving ourselves the grace to heal. We can build our confidence by taking small, consistent steps: questioning the negative thoughts that arise, practising self-compassion, and creating environments where we feel valued and supported.

You don't have to be defined by your past. Your confidence is still within you, waiting to be rediscovered. It takes time and effort, but with each step you take towards healing, your confidence will grow stronger. Your brain, your emotions, and your self-belief can all be reformed. Healing is possible, and so is a future where you believe in yourself, trust your instincts, and stand confidently in your worth.

CHAPTER 3

The Core of Confidence

3.1 Your Core Confidence: Always Within You

Have you ever had a moment when you looked at yourself in the mirror and wondered, Who am I really? Maybe it was after a failure, a betrayal, or a period of intense struggle. Or perhaps it was after a lifetime of quiet self-doubt, wondering if you were enough. It's easy to feel lost, disconnected from the woman you once were or the woman you know you're meant to be. You feel like the person looking back at you is not the whole, confident woman you were born to be. But let me share something incredibly powerful: **the confidence you seek is already inside you. It was never gone.**

It may seem impossible to believe when you're in the thick of self-doubt when your confidence has been eroded by circumstances beyond your control. But the truth is, your confidence is part of who you are. It's woven into the very fabric of your being. It's a gift from the Creator that no hardship, failure, or mistake can take away. It is deep inside of you, just waiting to be rediscovered.

In the Bible, we are told in **Genesis 1:27**, "So God created mankind in his own image, in the image of God he created them; male and female he created them." This verse is one of the most profound truths about your identity. You were created in the image of God. Do you understand the magnitude of that? You are made in the image of the flawless, perfect, and complete One.

This is not just a spiritual truth but a profound and foundational reality about who you are as a woman.

When God created you, He didn't make a mistake. He didn't look at you and think, Well, she's not quite enough, or She could use a little more of this or a little less of that. No, He created you perfect in His image — complete, flawless, and blameless. Your soul and spirit know this to be true. They know your worth, they know your strength, they know your beauty. It's your mind, your doubts, your fears that cloud this truth.

How many times have you told yourself that you weren't enough? How often have you compared yourself to others, thinking they had something you didn't? How many times have you felt you needed to prove your worth, either to others or even to yourself? This is the mind deceiving you. The mind takes the lies of the world — the judgments, the criticisms, the scars from past experiences — and wraps them around you like a blanket, convincing you that you're something less than what God created. But here's the thing: those lies are not your truth.

Your true confidence comes from knowing and accepting the truth of who you are. God made you in His image, and that image is whole, powerful, and beautiful. Your confidence is not tied to your achievements, your appearance, or the approval of others. It is tied to the unshakable truth that you were made by a Creator who loves you and calls you good and worthy.

Psalm 139:14 says, "I praise you because I am fearfully and wonderfully made; your works are wonderful, I know that full well." Let these words sink in. Fearfully and wonderfully made. That's you. **You are a reflection of God's craftsmanship, created with intention and care.** And the most powerful thing about this verse is that you are wonderfully made and know this full well. Your soul knows it. Your spirit knows it. It is embedded in your DNA, the essence of who you are.

But sometimes, we forget. We forget because life has a way of telling us that we're not enough. Relationships, disappointments, and the world's harsh expectations create stories in our minds that say, "If only I were more this or less that, I'd be worthy." We get so caught up in trying to meet external standards and prove ourselves to others that we lose sight of the truth that we were made perfect, just as we are.

It's not that our confidence was ever gone — it was buried under layers of doubt, fear, and external pressure. We've been taught to look for validation outside of ourselves, to tie our worth to fleeting and conditional things. But the truth is, **you don't need external validation to be confident.** Your confidence is rooted in something far deeper. It's rooted in the simple, powerful truth that you are created by God, in His image, with all the beauty and strength that comes with it. Your confidence is as intrinsic to you as your breath and heartbeat.

When I began to embrace this truth, my life began to change. I started to realise that confidence isn't about perfection—it's about authenticity. It's not about living up to the world's standards or the expectations of others. It's about living in alignment with the truth of who you are. You don't need to chase after confidence; you need to return to it, remember it, and uncover the confidence that is already inside you.

I want you to take a moment and reflect on this truth: **You are not broken. You are not unworthy. You were made to be whole, powerful, and confident, just as you are.** The pain, scars, and doubts don't define you.

They are part of your story, but they are not the end of your story. The end of your story is your reclaiming of your confidence, your reconnection with your true self.

This journey is not easy. It requires facing the lies we've been told, the wounds we've carried, and the fears that have held us back. But as you begin to uncover the truth about yourself, your confidence will return stronger than before. It's always been there. You were made for greatness, for power, for beauty. You are fearfully and wonderfully made. And you don't have to prove your worth to anyone.

Your confidence was never gone. It was just waiting for you to remember it. And now, it's time to reclaim it.

3.2 Rediscovering Your Confidence

Have you ever had a moment when you thought, this is not who I am meant to be? Maybe it came after a difficult experience, a personal failure, or a moment when you felt disconnected from the woman you thought you were. In those moments, it's easy to feel like something essential has been lost — like you're no longer the person you were meant to be. But what if I told you that nothing about you has been lost? What if I told you that the essence of who you are — your core confidence, your inner strength — is still there, just waiting to be rediscovered?

In this chapter, I want to introduce you to rediscovering your core of confidence. This process is about reconnecting with the true version of yourself that you might have forgotten or buried over the years. It's not about creating a new you; it's about uncovering the woman who has always been there—complete, capable, and worthy of all the dreams she holds.

You might wonder, how do we go about rediscovering our true selves when life, trauma, and self-doubt have shaped so much of our identity? How do we return to that place of unshakable confidence, where we can truly say I am enough? The answer lies in understanding the mind-body connection, the role of reprogramming, and, most importantly, in understanding your relationship with your true self.

The Neuroscience of Rediscovery: Reprogramming the Mind

Our brains are incredibly powerful, and they are constantly being shaped by our experiences. Neuroscience shows us that our minds are not static; they are malleable, continually rewiring based on the thoughts and experiences we expose them to. The term for this brain rewiring is neuroplasticity—the brain's ability to form new connections, strengthen existing ones, and even change the way it processes information.

What this means for you is that your mind, despite all the negative experiences and self-doubt you've experienced, has the ability to change. Just as old, limiting beliefs were learned, so can new, empowering beliefs take root. Through conscious effort and practice, you can reprogram your brain to reconnect with your true self — the self that was always whole, confident, and worthy.

Chapter Five will dive deeper into the **ACE framework**, a step-by-step process for reclaiming your confidence. This framework is designed to help you clear away the layers of doubt and fear and connect with your core confidence.

We will use **Awareness, Care, and Expression** to help you rebuild your confidence from the inside out. But before we get there, it's important to explore something foundational: the concept of SELF — and why it's crucial to understand which part of yourself you are nurturing.

The Self: The Soul, the Mind, and the Ego

William Shakespeare, the great playwright, famously said, "This above all: to thine own self be true, and it must follow, as the night the day, thou canst not then be false to any man." But what did he mean by self? Shakespeare's words resonate because they remind us that we must be true to ourselves. But which self are we being true to?

I believe Shakespeare was referring to the **spirit self**, the essence of who we are, our truest form — the part of us that is untouchable, unchanging, and full of infinite worth. The spirit self is the part of us aligned with truth, beauty, and confidence. It is the woman God created in His image — complete, perfect, and worthy. It's the part of you that knows, deep down, that you are capable of amazing things, regardless of what's happened to you. The spirit self is the core of your confidence.

Now, let's contrast this with something else Jesus said, a deeply transformative message: "If any of you want to be my followers, you must deny yourself." (Matthew 16:24). To which "self" is He referring? I believe Jesus refers to the **mind self** — the ego, the part of us constantly seeking external validation, approval, and recognition. The mind self is where fear, self-doubt, and false beliefs live.

It is the part of you that holds onto the pain from your past and tells you that you're not enough. The mind self wants you to believe that your worth is based on your job, relationships, or how others perceive you. But that's a lie.

The key to rediscovering your core confidence lies in understanding the difference between these two selves: the spirit self, which is flawless, complete, and in line with your highest purpose, and the mind self, which constantly tries to convince you that you're unworthy or broken.

The Power of Self-Connection

Confidence, at its core, is **about engaging in life from a place of worthiness**. It's about connecting with the spirit self, the part of you that knows you are enough, just as you are. It's about waking up every morning and thinking, I am enough, No matter what gets done and how much is left undone. It's going to bed at night and feeling the warmth of knowing that even though you are imperfect, vulnerable, and sometimes afraid, you are still brave, worthy of love, and deserving of belonging.

The relationship you have with yourself shapes every aspect of your life. The dreams you pursue, the relationships you create, and the peace you experience are all reflections of how much you embrace and value your true self. When you are connected to your core, to the confident woman you were born to be, everything else falls into place. The job you desire, the life partner you deserve, the ability to feel amazing in your own skin — these are all byproducts of the relationship you have with yourself.

As we move through this process of rediscovery, I want you to remember that confidence doesn't come from achieving external validation or perfection. It comes from engaging in your life from a place of inner worth. It comes from connecting with your spirit self, the one who is unshakeable, unbreakable, and whole. That is the confidence that you have always had inside you.

And now, it's time to reclaim it.

The First Step: Acknowledge Your Spirit Self

The first step to rediscovering your confidence is acknowledging your spirit self. The next step is trusting that your spirit self already knows who you are, what you're capable of, and what you deserve. In the coming chapters, we will explore how to clear away the layers of fear and doubt so that you can start living from your true, confident self.

But for now, take a moment to reflect on this: **You were made for greatness.** You are already enough. You are already complete. Confidence at your core is about reconnecting with that truth and moving forward with the courage, compassion, and self-belief to know that you are worthy of everything your heart desires.

Your confidence was never gone. It's just waiting for you to embrace it, to reconnect with the spirit self that has always been there, quietly reminding you of your unshakable worth. It's time to rediscover that core of confidence. It's time to remember who you truly are.

3.3 Reclaiming Confidence After Years of Doubt

I remember the weight of it all — the constant pressure to be perfect, keep everything together, and be the person everyone else expected me to be. It felt like an unspoken rule: Everything would fall into place if I could be perfect. But perfection, I've come to understand, is a mirage — something we chase but can never truly grasp. And as I relentlessly pursued that elusive ideal, it slowly started to wear me down in ways I didn't even realise at first.

It wasn't just my emotional and mental health that took a toll. My physical health began to suffer, too. I ignored the signs and pushed through the fatigue, the anxiety, and the overwhelming need to keep up appearances. I buried my feelings, drove away the fear, and told myself that if I just worked harder, achieved more, and kept smiling, I could somehow outrun the cracks forming inside me.

Then, one day, I felt it. A lump. At first, I brushed it off, thinking it was nothing — a temporary passing discomfort. But when it didn't go away, when it lingered and grew, I knew something was wrong. After all the years of carrying the weight of self-doubt, perfectionism, and fear, I had reached a breaking point. The lump in my breast was more than just a health scare; it was a wake-up call. It was as though my body was screaming at me, saying, Enough. Something had to change.

The fear that came with the diagnosis — the thought of cancer, of losing my health, of losing control — shook me to my core. But in that moment, something shifted. For the first time in a long time, I stopped trying to outrun the pain. I allowed myself to feel, confront, and listen to it. And that's when I realised that this journey of reclaiming my confidence wouldn't be a sprint.

It was going to be a relay, a gradual, step-by-step process. **One step at a time.**

I think that's the hardest part of reclaiming confidence after years of doubt: learning to let go of the race. For so long, I had been running, trying to keep up with an ideal of perfection that didn't even belong to me. But confidence, true confidence, isn't about the destination. It's about the journey — taking small, meaningful steps toward healing, self-acceptance, and embracing who you are, imperfections and all.

I realised that I didn't need to be perfect to be worthy, that I didn't need to have it all figured out to be enough. It was a painful, sometimes frustrating realisation but also liberating. I started to heal not just from the fear of cancer but also from the years of perfectionism that had held me captive. I allowed myself to be vulnerable, to admit that I wasn't okay and had been running on empty for far too long.

This journey of rediscovering my confidence wasn't linear. There were days when I felt like I had taken two steps forward, only to feel like I was falling three steps back. But with each step, no matter how small, I was reclaiming a piece of myself that I had lost along the way — the piece that believed in my worth, strength, and ability to rise above the doubts that had once consumed me.

And let me tell you, there's power in taking those small steps. The truth is that confidence is a process, not a destination. It's about being willing to stand up, day after day, and remind yourself that you are enough — even when it feels like the world is telling you otherwise. It's about making peace with your imperfections, embracing your flaws, and understanding that vulnerability is not a weakness but a strength.

Reclaiming confidence meant breaking free from believing I had to be perfect. It meant learning to take one step at a time, trusting that each step, no matter how small, was part of a bigger journey—a journey toward healing, self-acceptance, and a deeper understanding of who I truly was.

As I continued on that journey, I found that the fear that once controlled me started to fade. I began to trust myself again, to believe that I was worthy of good things, and to finally let go of the need to be perfect. I learned that true confidence comes from within, from embracing who you are, from owning your story— the good, the bad, and everything in between.

If there's one thing I want you to take away from this, it's this: confidence is not something you find. It's something you reclaim. It's already inside you, waiting to be rediscovered. And it doesn't come from perfection. It comes from the courage to show up as you are — imperfect and vulnerable but undeniably worthy of all the love, joy, and success you desire.

Healing, like confidence, is not a race. It's a journey. And with each step you take, you're reclaiming more of the powerful, beautiful, confident woman you've always been. You are enough. You've always been enough. And the best part? You're just getting started.

3.4 Your Confidence Is Covered, Not Destroyed

So many women, myself included, have believed that our confidence was shattered at one point or another — that it was lost for good. We've been through tough experiences, whether it's abuse, toxic relationships, or the weight of perfectionism. And somewhere along the way, we began to think that maybe, just maybe, our confidence was something we would never get back. But here's the truth I want you to understand: your confidence was never destroyed. It was covered up by layers of hurt, fear, and doubt. Beneath those layers, it still exists, waiting for you to rediscover it.

I remember feeling like my confidence was gone forever. After years of abuse, disappointment, and struggling to live up to impossible standards, I honestly thought I had lost who I was. But as I began to peel back the layers of fear and hurt, I realised something powerful: my true confidence was always there. It had never left me. It had just been buried under the pain of the past. It was there in my heart, waiting to be uncovered. And the same is true for you. **Your confidence is not gone. It's just hidden, waiting for you to dig through the layers and uncover it again.**

The first step in this process is cultivating **shame resilience**. This is key to reclaiming your power and self-worth. Shame is a silent killer of confidence. It convinces us that we are unworthy, unlovable, and broken. It makes us feel like we have to hide like we don't deserve to show up as our true selves. But the reality is that shame thrives in secrecy. It keeps us locked in a cycle of self-doubt and isolation. When we allow ourselves to be vulnerable and let others see our struggles and imperfections, we begin to break the power of shame. We let go of the lie that we are unworthy and allow ourselves to embrace the truth that we deserve love, respect, and happiness.

This is where vulnerability becomes so crucial. Vulnerability is often seen as a weakness in a world that values perfection and strength. But in reality, **vulnerability is the origin point for so much more.**

It is the foundation for innovation, adaptability, accountability, and visionary leadership. When we allow ourselves to be vulnerable, we open the door to creativity and growth. We allow ourselves to try new things, take risks, and evolve in ways we never thought possible. When we embrace vulnerability, we begin to understand our true strength.

I'll be honest: embracing vulnerability was not easy for me. For so long, I used perfectionism as a shield, hiding behind the illusion that if I could be perfect, no one would see my flaws, weaknesses, or fears. I believed that if I was perfect, I would be safe — from judgment, failure, and the pain of vulnerability. But the truth is that perfectionism is nothing more than a defence mechanism. It's an emotional armour we use to protect ourselves from the very thing we need to face: vulnerability.

Perfectionism, numbing, and other tactics we use to avoid feeling vulnerable are **emotional armour.** We wear these shields to protect ourselves from the fear of being judged, the fear of failure, and the fear of feeling like we're not enough. But these tactics don't truly protect us. They just keep us stuck. They keep us from feeling the full range of emotions that make us human — from experiencing joy, feeling deeply connected to others, and reclaiming our true confidence.

Perfectionism tells us we must be flawless, but it's an illusion. No one is perfect. We are all beautifully imperfect, which makes us so powerful. The real strength comes when we embrace our vulnerability, acknowledge our imperfections, and allow ourselves to be seen in all our raw, beautiful, messy glory.

Vulnerability is where true transformation happens. It's where we find the courage to face our fears, speak our truth, and take the next step in our healing journey.

When we embrace vulnerability, we begin to step into our power. We start to realise that our worth isn't tied to perfection but to the courage to show up as we are—with all of our flaws, struggles, and strengths.

In my journey, I learned that confidence doesn't come from being perfect or having everything together. It comes from embracing who I am, flaws and all. It comes from saying I am enough — even when I'm afraid and don't have all the answers. The more I allowed myself to be vulnerable, the more I rediscovered my confidence. I realised that true confidence is about accepting yourself fully, including your imperfections, and knowing you are still worthy of love, respect, and success.

The path to reclaiming your confidence is not about being perfect. It's about peeling back the layers of shame, fear, and self-doubt and allowing yourself to see the truth: you are worthy, capable, and beautiful, inside and out. As you begin to embrace vulnerability, you will begin to feel a new sense of strength and power that you've never known before.

So, as you continue on this journey, **I encourage you not to hide from your vulnerability**. Embrace it. Let it be the birthplace of your transformation. Let it be the fuel for your innovation, your growth, and your leadership. And as you do, you will find that your confidence, which has always been inside you, will rise and shine brighter. You were never broken. You were just hiding. Now, it's time to come out and show the world the powerful, confident woman you are.

CHAPTER 4

The Link Between Confidence and Power

4.1 Confidence and Personal Power: The Deep Connection

Confidence and power are often viewed as separate concepts as if they exist on opposite ends of a spectrum. Power is seen as external—something you have because of your position, accomplishments, or influence. Confidence, on the other hand, is seen as something more personal and internal—a feeling of self-assurance that comes from knowing your worth.

But as I've learned in my own life, **confidence and power are intricately connected,** and they cannot exist without each other. Confidence is not just about feeling good about yourself; it's about stepping into your personal power and knowing that you have everything you need within you to navigate the challenges life throws your way. Personal power doesn't come from external validation or success; it comes from within, from the quiet, unshakable belief that you are worthy and capable, no matter what.

This book, Confidence: Reclaim Your Power, One Step at a Time, is deeply personal. It represents the culmination of everything I've learned over the past ten years on my own healing journey, as well as the lessons I've witnessed in the lives of the incredible women around me. For so long, I thought I was just surviving — trying to piece together the broken fragments of my life. But as I've worked through the layers of self-doubt, fear, and shame, I've come to realise that the very act of reclaiming my confidence has been a powerful act of stepping into my own power.

Writing this book has been one of the most vulnerable experiences of my life. Each page, each word, is an invitation to look at the ways I've healed, the ways I've grown, and the ways I've stumbled and gotten back up. It's a way of bringing my personal story into the light, not for attention or validation, but to share the strength that has allowed me to transform my pain into power. It is a testament to the healing that is possible when you choose to embrace your worth and reclaim your confidence.

And that's what I want you to understand: **your confidence is your power.** When you feel confident, you tap into a wellspring of strength that allows you to take risks, stand up for what you believe in, and show up in the world as your authentic self. Confidence is not just a feeling; it's an act of choice—a decision to own your value, trust your instincts, and step into your full potential.

But let's be real. Confidence is not something that just magically appears one day. It's something you reclaim step by step. It's a practice that requires vulnerability, courage, and, above all, self-trust. It felt impossible When I started my journey to reclaim my confidence. I had spent many years trying to measure up to external expectations and living under the shadow of others' opinions. I thought I would feel powerful if I could just be perfect.

But the truth was, my perfectionism kept me stuck, afraid of failure and being seen for who I truly was. I hid behind a mask, pretending to be someone I wasn't to keep the peace and avoid rejection.

It wasn't until I started embracing my imperfections and allowed myself to be vulnerable and real that I began to experience true confidence. And with that confidence came a newfound sense of personal power. I no longer needed the approval of others to feel worthy. I no longer felt I had to prove myself or hide behind a perfect image. I understood that my power came from within — from the acceptance of myself, from the belief that I had the strength to overcome whatever challenges life threw at me.

And here's the thing: when you reclaim your confidence, you unlock your **personal power.** Confidence gives you the courage to speak your truth, set boundaries, and take ownership of your life. It helps you stop shrinking and start expanding into the fullness of who you are. It's not about being perfect. It's about being authentic. When you embrace who you truly are—with all your flaws, dreams, and fears—you become unstoppable.

Writing this book is about sharing what I've learned and, more importantly, using my own journey as a reminder that **we are all capable of stepping into our power.** We can all reclaim our confidence, no matter how lost we feel or how broken we think we are. It's about recognising that the power you seek is already inside you — it's just waiting for you to claim it.

The truth is reclaiming confidence isn't a one-time event. It's a process — a lifelong journey. But with every step you take, you become more attuned to the power that already resides within you.

As you continue this journey, you'll see that the confidence you're building is not just about feeling good at the moment; it's about creating a life that aligns with the woman you were always meant to be. A woman who knows her worth stands tall in her truth and leads with love, grace, and strength.

When I began embracing my confidence and personal power, I realised something profound: it wasn't just about me. Confidence is not just an individual experience; it is a collective one. When we, as women, step into our power, we transform our lives and the world around us. We become leaders, visionaries, and changemakers — not because we're perfect, but because we are brave enough to be vulnerable, courageous enough to be authentic, and powerful enough to rise above our circumstances.

And so, my invitation to you is this: **step into your power.** Reclaim your confidence, one step at a time. Know that the strength and power you seek are already inside you—they always have been. Your journey to rediscovering your confidence is about uncovering that power, embracing your true self, and showing up fully in the world—imperfect, authentic, and unshakably confident. Your power is waiting for you. It's time to claim it.

4.2 How Confidence Helps Women Take Control of Their Lives

For so many women, the journey to confidence is closely tied to the journey of vulnerability. It's not something we are often encouraged to embrace. In fact, we usually associate vulnerability with the emotions we want to avoid — fear, shame, uncertainty. We've been taught to hide those emotions, push them down, and protect ourselves from the discomfort they bring. And yet, the very thing we've been avoiding — vulnerability — is also the source of so much of the power, joy, and purpose we long for in our lives.

Think about it. When we allow ourselves to be vulnerable, we step into our truth. We no longer hide behind the walls of perfectionism or the masks we've worn to protect ourselves from being judged. We allow ourselves to feel, experience, and connect in deeply authentic ways. When we let go of the armour we've built over time, we can show up fully in our lives, be seen for who we truly are, and take control of our destiny.

This is where true confidence comes in. Confidence isn't about being perfect or flawless. It's about being courageous enough to face our vulnerability and choose to show up anyway. It's about standing in our truth, even when it feels uncomfortable and even when it challenges us to be honest about our fears, desires, and needs.

For me, this journey of reclaiming confidence was a process of learning to trust myself again — and learning that it was okay to be vulnerable. For so long, I believed that to be confident, I had to have everything figured out to look like I had all the answers. But as I began to lean into my vulnerability, I realised that **confidence is not about knowing all the answers; it's about being willing to ask the questions.** It's about allowing yourself to not know, stumble, and make mistakes without losing sight of your worth.

When we stand in our truth, we stop hiding behind the fear of judgment. We stop trying to meet the unrealistic expectations of others. We begin to live from a place of authenticity. And that, my dear friend, is where real power is found.

This is where the magic happens: **confidence allows us to assert our boundaries.** For too long, many have been afraid of setting boundaries, saying no, and speaking up for ourselves. We've been conditioned to be "nice," to people-please, to always put others' needs before our own. But the truth is, setting boundaries isn't selfish; it's essential for our well-being. It's how we protect our energy, our time, and our emotional health.

When we build our confidence, we realise that our needs matter. We begin to understand that it is not only okay to say no to things that drain us but also necessary for our growth and peace. The ability to assert our boundaries comes from knowing that we are worthy of respect, that our time and energy are valuable, and that we have the right to protect ourselves from anything or anyone compromising our well-being. This is not just an act of self-preservation; it is an act of self-love.

But here's the catch: when we allow ourselves to be vulnerable and open ourselves up to the discomfort of setting boundaries and speaking our truth, we also invite experiences that bring **purpose and meaning** to our lives. Vulnerability is the birthplace of **joy, belonging, creativity, authenticity, and love.** When we drop the armour and let go of the walls we've built to protect ourselves, we open ourselves to the beauty of human connection, the freedom of self-expression, and the joy of living in alignment with our truest selves.

I remember a time in my life when I had become so used to hiding my truth, so afraid to be vulnerable that I couldn't even speak up for what I needed. My personal and professional relationships were shaped by my fear of conflict and rejection. I wanted to be liked and accepted, so I never set boundaries, said no, or asked for what I needed.

I thought that if I could just be what others wanted me to be, I would finally be loved and respected.

But the truth was, I wasn't being true to myself. I wasn't allowing others to truly see me, and I wasn't allowing myself to show up authentically. It wasn't until I started to embrace vulnerability and own my truth that I began to find the courage to set boundaries, say no, and take control of my life. I started to create relationships built on mutual respect and honesty, not on fear or the need for approval.

When we step into our power and choose to stand in our truth, we are no longer controlled by fear, shame, or insecurity. We are empowered to take control of our lives and make choices that are aligned with our deepest values, desires, and needs. Confidence is not a magic switch that we flip overnight. It's a practice, a daily choice to show up, speak up, and love ourselves enough to say, "I am worthy of what I desire."

So, as you continue your journey of reclaiming confidence, I encourage you to **embrace vulnerability.** Don't be afraid to let go of the armour. Don't be scared to feel, to be seen, and to stand in your truth. Your confidence is directly linked to your willingness to show up as you truly are—imperfect, messy, beautiful, and worthy of everything your heart desires.

Vulnerability is not weakness. It is your strength. It is the source of your power. And it is the key to unlocking the life, love, and joy you've always been worthy of.

4.3 Women Who Unlocked Their Power Through Confidence

It's easy to look at other women and think that they've always had it figured out — that they've always been confident, always had the power to walk into a room and own it. But the truth is, many of these women have faced their own struggles, doubts, and fears. What sets them apart is not some inherent quality they were born with but their willingness to embrace their vulnerability, confront their fears, and choose confidence, one step at a time.

I've been privileged to meet many women whose stories have inspired me, and I want to share a few of their journeys with you because I know you can relate to their struggles deep down. More importantly, I want you to see how their confidence didn't come from perfection or a smooth path but from their courage to reclaim their power step by step.

Maria: The Woman Who Learned to Say No

Maria's story is one of reclaiming power through boundaries. She had spent the majority of her life people-pleasing. Always the first to help, always the one to say yes, Maria had become the go-to person for everyone else. Her friends, family, and colleagues relied on her, and she couldn't bear to disappoint them. The problem? She had nothing left for herself. Her needs were always at the bottom of her list, and deep down, she became resentful.

Maria was working in a high-pressure job when everything came to a head. She had been assigned an important project that required long hours and significant personal sacrifices.

One evening, exhausted and overwhelmed, Maria realised she couldn't keep going like this. She wasn't just burnt out; she was losing herself in the process.

It was then that Maria realised she had to choose to either continue to let others dictate her time, energy, and boundaries or take control and honour her needs. That moment was the turning point for her. Maria started to say no. She stopped accepting last-minute requests and set clear boundaries with her family and friends. It wasn't easy. There were moments of guilt, fear, and doubt. But she stood firm. She realised that she wasn't selfish in taking care of herself. In fact, setting boundaries was the most powerful thing she could do for herself and the people around her.

As Maria began honouring her time and energy, she felt her confidence grow. She wasn't waiting for validation from others. She was learning to trust herself, to trust that her needs mattered just as much as anyone else's. And with each boundary she set, her power — her true power — became more apparent.

Ella: The Survivor Who Found Her Voice

Ella's journey was **healing from trauma** and rediscovering her inner voice. She had spent years in an abusive marriage, trapped in a cycle of emotional manipulation and control. She had been told she was unworthy, unloved, and not enough. Her confidence had been shattered by the constant criticisms, the gaslighting, and the silent treatment. Over time, Ella had stopped believing in herself. She had stopped speaking up, stopped standing up for what she wanted, and began to shrink in every area of her life.

It wasn't until Ella's marriage ended that she started to confront the truth. She realised that she had been living in the shadow of someone else's version of her — and that version was distorted, filled with lies and manipulation. Ella had to reclaim her voice. The first time she spoke her truth out loud — to a therapist or close friend — it felt like an explosion inside her. It was terrifying, raw, and vulnerable. But it was also the beginning of her transformation.

She learned to trust herself again. Ella began speaking up for what she wanted, making decisions for herself without seeking permission from others. With each step, she realised her power wasn't in pleasing others or staying small. Her power was in her authenticity — her ability to speak her truth, no matter how difficult or scary it felt.

Now, Ella advocates for herself and others who have faced similar struggles. She has used her voice to empower other women, to help them rediscover their worth, and to encourage them to step into their own power.

Tasha: The Entrepreneur Who Stopped Hiding

Tasha's story is one of **embracing vulnerability** and stepping into leadership. Tasha had always been an incredible woman. She was smart, driven, and had an entrepreneurial spirit that could light up any room. But for years, she hid behind self-doubt, afraid of stepping fully into her potential. She ran a small business but kept it small because she feared success. She was terrified of the attention, the responsibility, and the scrutiny that might come with it.

What changed for Tasha was an honest conversation with a mentor, who asked her point-blank, "Why aren't you going for it?" The question hit her hard. Why wasn't she? She realised that her fear of vulnerability — of being seen and judged — had been holding her back. She had believed that vulnerability was a weakness, something to be avoided at all costs. But Tasha began to understand that vulnerability is actually the birthplace of strength. It's where innovation is born, creativity flows, and true leadership comes from.

Tasha started to show up authentically in her business. She shared her struggles, lessons, and triumphs with her clients. She became more visible, open, and honest about who she was and what she was building. And with that authenticity, her business grew. She began attracting clients who resonated with her true self, not the polished, perfect version she had been trying to present for so long.

Tasha found her power when she allowed herself to be vulnerable. She realised her confidence wasn't about being perfect or having all the answers. It was about showing up, imperfections, and trusting that she was enough — exactly as she was.

These women — Maria, Ella, and Tasha — prove that reclaiming your confidence is not just about feeling good in the moment. It's about taking control of your life. It's about **standing in your truth,** asserting your boundaries, and stepping into your personal power. It's about vulnerability, embracing imperfections, and knowing **you are worthy of everything you desire.**

Like you, they had to take one step at a time, making the choice to believe in themselves, to trust that their confidence was always there—waiting to be uncovered. They reclaimed their power by being brave enough to show up authentically, even when it was hard. And through that authenticity, they found their strength.

So, I ask you now: What are you holding back? What parts of yourself have you been hiding? The world is waiting for you to step into your power. Your confidence is ready to be reclaimed. And just like Maria, Ella, and Tasha, you have everything you need within you to unlock your full potential. It's time to rise, to stand in your truth, and to reclaim your power — one step at a time.

4.4 The Inner Strength Found in Embracing Confidence

One song often comes to mind when I reflect on my past: "It Wasn't Me" by Shaggy. Now, it sounds strange to tie a lighthearted, catchy tune to such a deeply transformative journey, but bear with me. The song tells the story of a man caught in a compromising situation and, despite all evidence pointing to the truth, denies it, repeatedly saying, "It wasn't me." There's something in that constant denial — that refusal to face reality — that resonates with so many of us regarding our confidence.

For so long, I lived like that — denying my true self, pushing away the parts of me that I thought weren't good enough, and constantly hiding behind the expectations I felt I had to meet. I was caught in a loop of trying to be someone I wasn't, ignoring the truth of who I was beneath all the layers of fear, doubt, and perfectionism.

But here's the twist: **embracing your confidence** is like coming to the realisation in that song—it's acknowledging the truth that you are enough. It's saying, "This is who I am. This is the real me, without excuses, fear, or shame." And it is incredibly powerful. **It is freedom.**

This journey of rediscovering confidence is a lot like what the Bible speaks of when it says, "If anyone is in Christ, the person is a new creature" (2 Corinthians 5:17). It's a moment of renewal, of stepping into the truth of who you were always meant to be. It's like putting on a new set of eyes, seeing yourself with the clarity that comes from understanding that you were never broken, never unworthy. You were always whole, always capable.

Embracing your confidence means embracing your spirit self — the part of you that is pure, unblemished, and strong. Your spirit is the essence of who you are — the one God created and who was made in His image, complete and perfect. It is from this place that your true strength comes.

When you stop hiding, denying your worth, and embracing the woman you were meant to be—with all her beauty, strength, flaws, and authenticity—you tap into a wellspring of inner strength and resilience. Your confidence is not just a feeling; it is a reminder that you are capable of overcoming anything life throws at you. It is the power to face challenges head-on, stand up for yourself, assert your boundaries, and rise after every fall.

Coming awake to your confidence is like peeling away layers of fear and insecurity. It's a slow, sometimes painful process of stripping away everything you've been told you should be and reconnecting with the truth of who you are—the truth that you are worthy, powerful, and resilient. The truth is that you have the strength to rise again, no matter how many times you fall.

For so long, I didn't understand the beauty of my own spirit — the beauty that was there all along, waiting to be acknowledged. But once I embraced my confidence, I faced the strength that lay dormant inside me. It wasn't a strength built on external validation, on achievements, or on the approval of others. It was a strength rooted in the belief that I am enough, exactly as I am. And that strength gave me the courage to rebuild, heal, and reclaim my life.

This is where **true resilience** comes from: not from denying our flaws, not from pretending to be perfect, but from embracing the beauty of our imperfections. It comes from accepting that we are worthy of everything life offers simply because we exist. When we embrace our confidence, we embrace our true self — the self who is whole, powerful, and free.

So, as you read these words, I want you to pause and reflect on the woman you are—the woman you've always been. Embrace the spirit within you, the one that has always been strong, always capable, always enough. Your confidence is not something you have to earn. It is already inside you, waiting to be rediscovered.

And when you start to live from this place — from the truth of who you are — you'll begin to see the beauty that was always intended for you. You'll see your power. You'll see your strength. You'll see a woman who is more than capable of achieving everything she desires. You'll see that your confidence is not just a part of you; it is the very core of who you were always meant to be.

CHAPTER 5

The Framework: Reclaiming Your Confidence (ACE)

In 2016, as I was deep into my transformative journey, I found myself journaling almost every day. I had started to track my progress — those little "aha" moments where I felt like I was truly waking up to the woman I was always meant to be. Deep down, these revelations were so powerful, raw, and incredibly personal that I knew they were meant to be shared. But something held me back. I felt it wasn't the right time. There were fears of not being perfect, of not having all the answers. And so, I kept it all to myself.

Looking back, I see that fear for what it was — a barrier. A barrier to owning my story, stepping into my power and sharing something that could help others. **It reminded me that embracing my confidence meant embracing the fact that I didn't have to be perfect.** I didn't need to wait until I had everything figured out. I needed to be vulnerable, to share the process, the messiness, and the beauty of it all.

So, here I am, sharing for the very first time my ACE transformative framework — the steps I used to reclaim my confidence, step by step, and the same framework I believe can help you do the same.

Figure 1: The ACE Framework

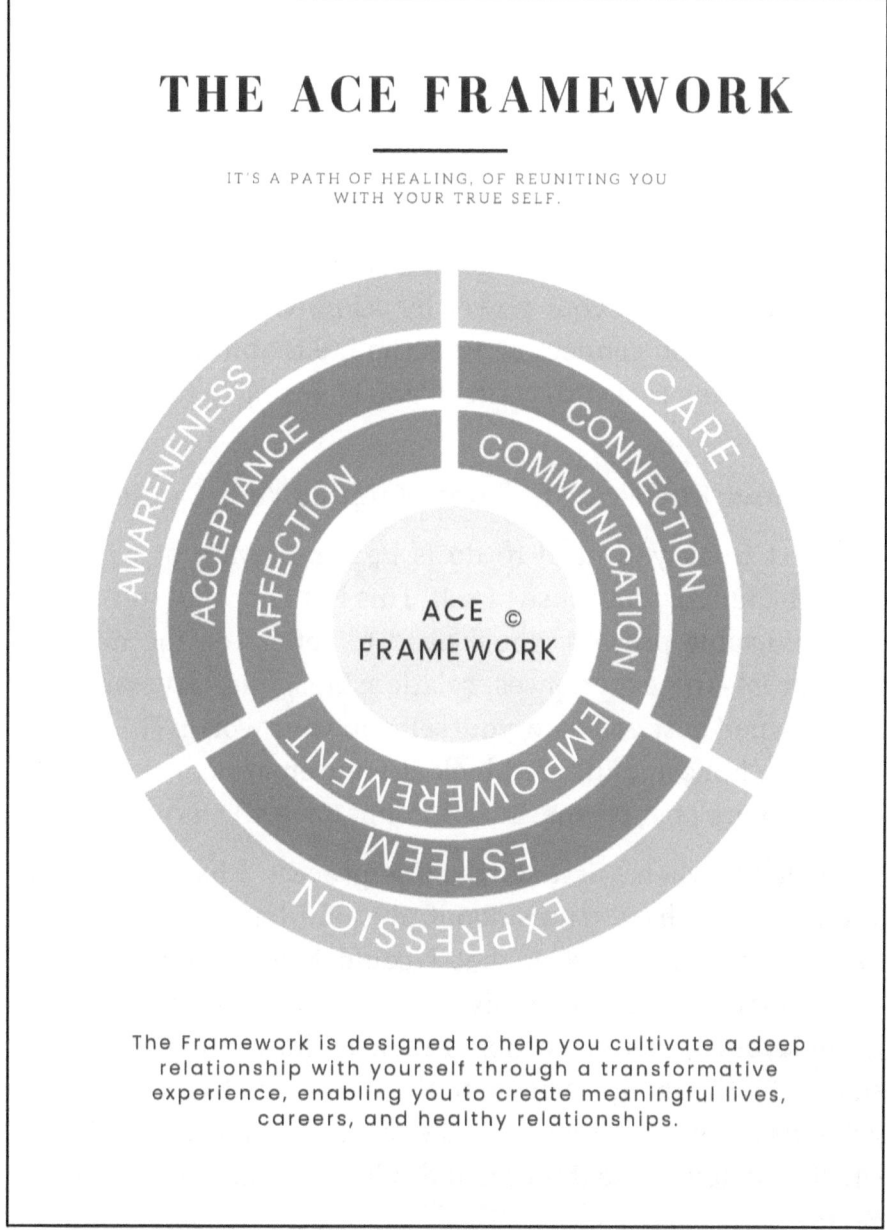

5.1 A – Awareness, Affection, Affirmation

The first step of the ACE framework is **A** — Awareness, Affection, and Affirmation. This step is about coming home to yourself. It's about stepping into your power by acknowledging the truth of who you are and connecting with the life that lives within you. It's about being real with yourself and choosing to take that first step into healing.

Awareness: The First Step to Reclaiming Your Confidence

The first thing you need to do is become aware of what has shaped your current sense of self. This is a deep and sometimes uncomfortable process. You'll need to reflect on the negative influences—the experiences, relationships, and traumas—that have shaped how you view yourself and your worth. This means taking an honest, unfiltered look at your emotional state at the places where fear, shame, or self-doubt have taken root.

I remember when I first started this process. I had to dig deep and face some hard truths about myself. I had lived so long in denial, convincing myself that I could keep moving forward without truly dealing with my past. But as I started to uncover those layers of self-protection, I realised how much I had been shaped by the things I had gone through. I had to recognise the patterns of toxic relationships, the ways I had been made to feel small, and how these things had eroded my confidence over the years.

It's easy to deny or ignore the past, especially when it's painful. But awareness is the key to unlocking the door to your true self. Only when you're willing to face the past — to see it for what it is — can you begin to heal and reclaim your confidence.

Affection: Showing Yourself Compassion

The next step is **Affection**. Once you've gained awareness, it's time to show yourself the compassion and care you deserve. This is where the real work begins: healing your confidence means embracing self-love and kindness. It's so easy to be hard on ourselves, to focus on what we've done wrong or what we think we lack. But this step concerns treating yourself with the same gentleness and care you would offer a dear friend.

For so long, I wasn't kind to myself. I was my own harshest critic. I would berate myself for the smallest mistakes, telling myself I wasn't enough and had failed. But when I started to show myself compassion — when I began to embrace the idea that I was worthy of love despite my flaws — something shifted. Self-compassion is the foundation of rebuilding your confidence because it allows you to forgive yourself and see yourself through the lens of love and understanding. You can't heal if you're constantly fighting against yourself.

To truly reclaim your confidence, you must learn to treat yourself with Affection, not only in moments of success but also in your struggles, fears, and imperfections. This isn't just about being kind to yourself in thought but also in action—in how you speak to yourself, care for your body and mind, and honour your needs.

Affirmation: Rebuilding Your Inner Dialogue

Finally, we come to **Affirmation**. Knowing your worth is not enough; you need to remind yourself of it daily. Affirmations are powerful because they remind you that you deserve love, respect, and confidence. They help rewire the negative thoughts and beliefs that have taken root over time.

When I first started using affirmations, it felt strange — almost like I was lying to myself. But over time, I realised that these positive affirmations were not about pretending everything was perfect. They were about affirming the truth of who I was. I began to replace the negative self-talk with empowering statements like, I am worthy of confidence, I am strong, and I am enough. The more I said them, the more I believed them.

Affirmations are not just words; they are declarations of your truth. They are powerful tools that can shift your mindset, reframe your beliefs, and rebuild your confidence. **Affirm your worth daily** — not just when you feel good, but especially on the days when you're struggling. Reaffirm that you are deserving of all the love, respect, and success that life has to offer.

The ACE framework is designed to take you on a journey of self-discovery, healing, and empowerment. It's about understanding that **confidence is not something you need to find outside of yourself;** it's something already inside you, waiting to be reclaimed.

By becoming aware of the negative influences in your life, showing yourself compassion, and affirming your worth, you can start to rebuild your confidence, one step at a time. You can learn to trust yourself again, to show up authentically, and to step into the life you were always meant to lead.

This is not a race; this is a journey. It's about taking each step with intention, love, and understanding that **you are worthy of**

this transformation. As you move through this process, remember that your confidence is not lost—it's always been there, waiting for you to reclaim it.

5.2 C – Care, Connection, Communication

Through my transformation, I learned something profound — the power of **care.** For so long, I had carried the weight of everything alone, convinced I had to be strong enough to handle it all. I didn't allow myself the luxury of vulnerability. I built walls around my heart, telling myself that if I could keep pushing through, I would be fine. But the truth is, strength doesn't come from shutting down; it comes from softening, from allowing ourselves to be held, to be cared for.

I remember the first time I allowed myself to truly **be held**. It wasn't just physical; it was an emotional and spiritual surrender. I began to understand what it meant to trust — to trust God, to trust myself, and to trust the process of healing. The Bible says, "All I require for life has been given" (2 Peter 1:3). This was a turning point for me. I began to embrace the truth that everything I needed to heal and thrive was already within my reach. I no longer had to carry the world's weight on my shoulders alone. I could lean on God, lean on those who loved me, and allow myself the care I had denied myself for so long.

When a woman feels supported, she starts to build trust — not only in others but in herself and in the process of life itself. She begins to remember that life is kind, that she is not alone in her struggles, and that she is worthy of love, care, and all the good things life offers. And from this place of trust, she reconnects with her true self. She starts to believe that life is in her favour and that the challenges she faces are not obstacles but opportunities for growth.

This **care** opens the door to **connection.** The more I cared for myself, the more I connected with my deeper self. This connection allowed me to see my mind in a different light. Rather than fighting against it, I learned to work with it. I began to understand how to train my thoughts and harness my mind's power to support rather than sabotage me.

Connection is about understanding ourselves and building relationships with others who encourage and uplift us. The relationships we keep shape who we are. I began to surround myself with people who believed in me, supported me, and encouraged me to keep growing. I sought out spaces where I felt accepted and understood. These connections were not just about external validation but about being in a space where I could be unfiltered and unashamed.

I remember the deep sense of relief when I first allowed myself to connect with others in a way that wasn't about performing or proving anything. It was just about being—being real, being vulnerable, and being supported. Those connections were the foundation for my healing. They gave me the courage to reconnect with my body, mind, and spirit. From this space of true connection, I began to realise the immense power within us all.

And then, there was **communication.** As I began to nurture my self-care and build meaningful connections, I realised that communicating was the next step in reclaiming my confidence. This isn't just about talking; it's about expressing my needs, boundaries, and emotions clearly. Communication is how we assert our value to the world. It is the bridge that connects us to others in meaningful ways.

I used to think that speaking up for myself meant being confrontational or demanding. But the more I embraced my true self, the more I understood that communication is about asserting your worth in a way that honours yourself and others. It's about creating a space where you can share your truth without fear of judgment, and others can do the same. It's about setting boundaries with kindness and compassion, ensuring you are valued and respected in every relationship.

Learning to communicate from the heart was one of the most transformative aspects of reclaiming my confidence. I stopped shrinking in conversations, stopped apologising for my needs, and stopped compromising my boundaries to make others comfortable. I began to speak my truth — even when it was hard and I felt vulnerable. And the more I did, the more my confidence grew. I learned that clear, honest communication creates a space for others to honour your truth, and in turn, it honours your own sense of self-worth.

The C of the ACE framework—care, Connection, and Communication—is a powerful trio that anchors your journey to reclaiming confidence. It's about taking the time to care for yourself, building relationships that nurture and support your growth, and communicating your needs with clarity and strength. This is how we reconnect with our true power.

When you care for yourself, connect with the right people, and communicate your needs and boundaries, you create a life that honours who you truly are. You begin to stand in your truth, assert your worth, and take control of your life. The power to reclaim your confidence lies in your ability to care for yourself, surround yourself with supportive, uplifting relationships, and communicate from a place of authenticity.

So, take the time to care for yourself physically, emotionally, and spiritually. Build those connections that help you grow and support you along the way. Most importantly, start communicating—express your truth, your boundaries, and your needs, knowing that you are worthy of all the love and respect the world has to offer.

5.3 E – Expression, Esteem, Empowerment

In my journey of reclaiming confidence, I realised something essential: **true confidence comes from expression, esteem, and empowerment.** These three elements are not separate from one another but interconnected, weaving a fabric that holds our authenticity and inner strength together. As I moved through my own process, I had to learn to step into my truth, awaken my heart, and give it permission to come out of hiding. It wasn't easy. For so long, I buried my feelings, desires, and dreams, afraid that if I expressed them, they wouldn't be welcomed or understood. But I learned that **expression is freedom.**

Each time I allowed myself to express what I felt, thought, and wanted, it felt like a piece of my soul was being set free. When I finally gave myself permission to express my emotions, it was as though the walls I had built around my heart began to crumble. I started to connect with myself in a way I never had before. Whether through journaling, art, or conversation, healthy expression became the channel through which I released suppressed emotions, the ones that had been silently weighing me down for so long.

Each word I wrote, each feeling I shared, became a form of self-expression. As I allowed myself to be more open and vulnerable, I realised that my actions — whether creating this book, a project or simply living each day — were no longer based on external pressures or the desire to please others.

They were divinely inspired, grounded in my true self, and not shaped by trends or popular opinion. I felt empowered by this new expression of myself. I could walk through the world unapologetically, knowing that everything I created was a version of me — my truth, my heart, my story.

Your confidence will grow exponentially when you give yourself permission to express your true self.

Expression: Give Yourself Permission to Be Free

Expression, in whatever form it takes, is a vital component of reclaiming your confidence. For me, it began with journaling. The simple act of writing down my thoughts, fears, and hopes helped me process and release emotions I hadn't even known I was holding onto. As I poured my heart onto paper, I began to understand myself more deeply. This process helped me connect with my own desires, needs, and true voice.

But expression doesn't have to be limited to journaling. It could be in art, music, dance, or simply speaking your truth with the people who matter. Whatever form of expression you choose is about allowing yourself to be seen. It's about no longer hiding your feelings or desires and, instead, giving yourself the space to fully be yourself. This is how you heal, how you grow, and how you build self-worth. Through expression, we begin to feel validated and recognise that our feelings, ideas, and voices matter.

Esteem: Recognise Your Value

When you express yourself authentically, you are actively building your self-esteem. Esteem is not about self-praise for every little thing you do but about recognising your inherent value — acknowledging that you are worthy, just as you are. I used to struggle with this — I would downplay my achievements, focusing only on what I hadn't done or where I still felt lacking. But I realised that self-esteem is built by recognising your value, no matter how small the achievement may seem.

In my journey, I started to celebrate the small wins: completing a challenging task, speaking up when I normally would have stayed silent, or simply being kind to myself on tough days. Every step forward counts; the more you affirm your worth, the stronger your confidence will grow. Remember, you are not the sum of your failures or mistakes; you are the sum of your efforts, growth, and perseverance. You are valuable just by being you.

Empowerment: Taking Action from Your Strength

Now, the third component—empowerment. This is where things start to shift in a big way. Confidence is not just about feeling strong; it's about taking action based on that strength. Empowerment is about realising that you can shape your own life, make decisions that reflect your values and beliefs, and step into the life you deserve.

For so long, I had felt powerless in certain areas of my life. I had let circumstances, people, and fears dictate my decisions. I had allowed doubt to cloud my judgment, convincing myself that I wasn't capable of acting from a place of strength. But as I began expressing my truth and building my self-esteem, I realised I could take control. I could make choices that reflected my worth. I could trust myself to step into challenging situations, knowing I was more than capable.

Empowerment comes when you begin to see yourself as the driver of your own life, not a passenger. It's when you stop waiting for permission to pursue your dreams and instead take bold, confident steps toward what you desire. Confidence is about acting on your beliefs and values, no matter how scary it feels. Every decision to move toward your authentic self is an act of empowerment. It's about trusting that you can handle whatever comes your way because you've already proven to yourself that you are strong, capable, and worthy.

As you embrace the **E** of the ACE framework — **Expression, Esteem, and Empowerment** — you will begin to see the layers of doubt and fear that have held you back start to melt away. You'll begin to express your truth, recognising your value and celebrating your worth. Your esteem will grow as you acknowledge your achievements, no matter how small, and begin to treat yourself with the care and respect you deserve. And most importantly, you will feel empowered to make decisions that align with your highest self, knowing you have everything you need to reach your fullest potential.

This journey is not about being perfect. It's about being real, bold, and trusting that the steps you take today will lead you to the confident, empowered woman you were always meant to be. Every word you speak, and action you take is a step toward reclaiming your confidence — ultimately empowering you to live the life you've always dreamed of.

CHAPTER 6

Your Confidence in Action

Although this is my first time publicly sharing the ACE framework, it is far from the first time I've used it. Over the years, whether I've been working with women through coaching, counselling, or leading teams, I've seen how powerful these steps can be. I've witnessed women transform their lives, rediscover their worth, and rise into the powerful, confident beings they were always meant to be.

This book is both a theory and a tool you can use, just as I have. I've shared the steps of the ACE framework, but I've also included **additional resources** in the appendix. These techniques help you **coach yourself** to continue your journey beyond these pages. You'll also find an assessment to rate your ACE level — a tool to track your progress and celebrate your growth. Reclaiming your confidence is a dynamic process, and this assessment will help you see where you are and where you need to go.

6.1 Women Who Have ACE'd Their Confidence

I want to share a few stories of women who have used the ACE framework to reclaim their confidence. These women came from different backgrounds and faced unique challenges, yet their journeys are connected by one thread: the courage to choose confidence, even in the face of fear, doubt, and hardship.

Ava's Story: From Self-Doubt to Leadership

Ava, a talented professional, spent years struggling with imposter syndrome. She was constantly second-guessing her abilities, afraid that someone would discover she wasn't as good as she appeared. She had achieved success in her career, but internally, she felt inadequate. She began using the ACE framework, starting with awareness. She recognised the negative self-talk that had plagued her for years — the belief that she wasn't worthy of the position she had worked so hard for. Ava committed to showing affection — practising self-compassion, and speaking kindly to herself. She reshaped her inner dialogue through affirmations, replacing self-doubt with the knowledge that she was capable, qualified, and deserving.

As she progressed through the steps, Ava noticed her confidence rise. She began to assert her boundaries at work, confidently voicing her needs and taking on leadership roles she would have once avoided. Her newfound confidence didn't just change how she felt about herself; it transformed how others saw her. Ava's story is a testament to the power of embracing your worth and stepping into your leadership, even when you feel the weight of doubt and fear.

Jasmine's Journey: Healing from Trauma

Jasmine's path to confidence was deeply rooted in healing from trauma. After a difficult divorce, Jasmine struggled with feelings of inadequacy and fear of never being enough. She had internalised so many of the painful words and actions from her past relationship that she couldn't see the woman she truly was anymore.

Starting with awareness, Jasmine began to unpack the beliefs planted in her mind during her marriage. She realised she had been living her life based on the false narrative that she was unworthy of love and happiness. Through self-care, she learned to nurture herself again, prioritising her emotional and physical health. She started to express her feelings and needs without fear of judgment, and through empowerment, she began to make decisions based on her newfound confidence.

Jasmine's transformation was not immediate, but every small step she took brought her closer to the confident, empowered woman she is today. She is now actively pursuing her dreams, leading a purposeful life, and modelling to her children what it means to live with self-respect and confidence.

Maya's Story: From Isolation to Connection

Maya, a mother of three, had spent years feeling isolated. She was so focused on caring for everyone else that she lost sight of her needs. Maya had lost touch with her confidence after years of suppressing her desires and living in the shadows of others' expectations. However, through the ACE framework, she could connect with herself again. She started expressing her needs, both in her family and in her professional life. Through esteem-building practices, she began to recognise her value and worth, regardless of the expectations placed on her.

Maya learned to empower herself by setting boundaries with her family and taking time for self-care. She started to connect with like-minded women who uplifted her and reminded her that she was not alone in her journey. Today, Maya lives a life filled with purpose and connection, no longer feeling isolated but supported and strong in her power.

While unique in their circumstances, these stories highlight a universal truth: reclaiming your confidence is possible, no matter your past or present situation. Every woman can rediscover her worth, rebuild her confidence, and rise into her power.

6.2 Sustaining Confidence in Daily Life

Reclaiming your confidence is just the beginning. The real work comes in sustaining and integrating it into every aspect of your life. Here are a few key practices to help you maintain your confidence:

1. **Daily Affirmations:** Start your day with powerful affirmations that remind you of your worth. These could be simple statements like, I am worthy of love, respect, and success or I trust myself to make empowered decisions. Reaffirming your worth daily strengthens your self-belief and sets the tone for your day.

2. **Set Boundaries:** Confidence is rooted in knowing and asserting your boundaries. Whether at work, in relationships, or with yourself, setting clear boundaries ensures that external pressures do not compromise your confidence. It's an act of self-respect and self-love.

3. **Self-Reflection:** Take time to reflect on your progress. Regular journaling or meditation allows you to check in with your emotional state and remind yourself of the steps you've taken toward reclaiming your confidence. Celebrate your small wins.

4. **Surround Yourself with Positive Influences:** The people you spend time with can lift or bring you down. Surround yourself with individuals who encourage, support, and inspire you to grow.

6.3 Reclaiming Confidence as an Ongoing Journey of Growth

I want to be clear: reclaiming confidence is not a destination. It is an ongoing journey of growth, self-discovery, and self-love. Life will always present new challenges; there will be moments of self-doubt, setbacks, and moments where you feel like you're not enough. But the beauty of reclaiming your confidence is that, even in those moments, you can choose to rise. You can choose to remember that your confidence is not dependent on perfection but on your ability to embrace your truth, imperfections and all.

Reclaiming confidence is about learning to love yourself more deeply with each step, trust yourself more fully, and show up for yourself, no matter what. It is about understanding that you are worthy of every good thing — and that confidence, like love, is an ongoing journey, not a one-time achievement.

6.4 An Empowering Message to Inspire You to Rise and Own Your Power

As I close this chapter, I want you to hear this truth: **You are more than enough.** Your journey to reclaim your confidence is uniquely yours, and you are the author of your story. Deep within you is everything you need to step into your power and live the life you deserve.

Remember, reclaiming your confidence isn't about being perfect — it's about being authentic. It's about embracing every part of you — your beauty, your flaws, your strength, and your vulnerability. You are deserving of love, respect, and success, and you are more than capable of achieving anything you set your heart on.

So, **rise. Rise into your power,** your confidence, and your truth. Embrace the woman you were always meant to be. And as you do, know that the world is waiting for you — the real, unapologetic, confident you. **This is your time.**

APPENDIX 1

Coaching Questions and Techniques for ACE

The following open-ended questions and techniques are designed to help you **coach yourself** through the ACE framework. These prompts are meant to challenge you, to help you explore your inner world, and to guide you as you reclaim your confidence. Don't rush through them — sit with each question, feel it deeply, and allow yourself to be vulnerable. This is where the real transformation happens.

A – Awareness, Affection, Affirmation

Awareness:

1. **What messages have I been telling myself about my worth and abilities?**
   Explore the roots of these beliefs. Where did they come from? Are they truly mine, or were they handed to me by others?

2. **How have my past experiences shaped the way I see myself today?**
   Reflect on the experiences — positive or negative — that have influenced your self-perception. What patterns do you see?

3. **In what areas of my life do I feel most disconnected from myself?**
   Notice where you've built walls, ignored your intuition or

denied your needs. What does that disconnection look like?

4. **What are the lies I've believed about myself?**
   What false stories have you been carrying? Are they still serving you? What would happen if you let them go?

Technique:
Write down your limiting beliefs and negative self-talk. Then, for each one, write a counter-affirmation rooted in your worth and strength. This is your personal declaration of truth.

Affection:

1. **How can I begin to show myself the same care and compassion I give to others?**
   Think of the kindness you extend to friends, family, and colleagues. How can you turn that compassion inward?

2. **What would it look like to forgive myself for past mistakes?**
   Let go of any guilt, shame, or regret you are holding. What happens when you truly forgive yourself?

3. **How can I learn to nurture my emotional needs without feeling selfish?**
   Allow yourself to receive care without guilt. What would it take to give yourself permission to feel nurtured?

4. **What parts of myself have I been neglecting or rejecting?**
   What do you hide or suppress in yourself? What would it mean to embrace those parts of you instead?

Technique:
Practice a self-compassion exercise: stand in front of a mirror, look into your own eyes, and say, *I love you, I see you, and I am here for you.* Repeat this every day for a week and notice the changes in your heart and mind.

Affirmation:

1. **What is the most empowering belief I could have about myself?**
   Imagine you have no limitations, no fears — what would you believe about yourself?

2. **What would it feel like to fully embrace my worth and stop apologising for taking up space?**
   What would change in your life if you showed up unapologetically as your true self?

3. **When I speak to myself, what tone am I using? Is it nurturing or critical?**
   Notice how you talk to yourself. How does your inner dialogue shift when you use kindness and encouragement instead of criticism?

4. **What positive affirmations can I say to myself every day that will challenge the doubts I've carried?**
   Pick one affirmation that speaks directly to your heart and commit to saying it daily. What does it feel like to say it aloud?

Technique:
Create a daily ritual where you speak your affirmations out loud. Stand tall, breathe deeply, and say the words with

conviction. Record yourself and listen to it each day to reinforce your belief in your power.

C – Care, Connection, Communication

Care:

1. **What is one thing I can do today to nurture myself?**
   Identify one small act of self-care you can commit to — whether it's a few minutes of deep breathing, a walk, or simply resting. What does this act of care tell you about your worth?

2. **What am I afraid will happen if I take care of myself more regularly?**
   What fears arise when you think about prioritising your well-being? Are they based on truth or fear?

3. **How can I create a daily routine that supports my mental, physical, and emotional well-being?**
   Imagine a day where you show up for yourself — what does it look like? What steps can you take to make it a reality?

4. **What does it mean to be 'worthy of care' in my own eyes?**
   How do you define self-worth in practical terms? How can you align your actions with that definition?

Technique:
Design a self-care plan that nurtures every aspect of your being. Schedule it in your calendar as a non-negotiable appointment with yourself. Let it be a reminder that your well-being matters.

Connection:

1. **Who are the people who uplift me and make me feel seen, heard, and understood?**
   Think of the people who bring out the best in you. How can you nurture these relationships?

2. **Where am I holding myself back from authentic connection?**
   In what ways are you limiting your relationships because of fear or past hurt? What would it look like to be more open?

3. **What does it mean to feel truly supported?**
   What does support look like to you? Is it physical, emotional, or both? How can you start creating a support network that nourishes your growth?

4. **How can I connect more deeply with my own soul?**
   What practices can you incorporate into your life that will allow you to connect more intimately with yourself?

Technique:
Reach out to a trusted friend or mentor and share something vulnerable. Let them hold space for you without judgment. Afterward, reflect on how it feels to allow yourself to be seen and supported.

Communication:

1. **When was the last time I communicated my needs clearly and confidently?**
   Reflect on a time when you asserted yourself. What went well? What could you improve?

2. **What does it feel like to express my boundaries without feeling guilty?**
   Think of a situation where you had to set a boundary. How did you feel afterward? What would it take to set that boundary with more ease next time?

3. **How do I communicate with myself in moments of self-doubt or fear?**
   When you're scared or unsure, what do you say to yourself? How can you start talking to yourself like a trusted friend instead?

4. **What is the most authentic way I can express myself to others?**
   Imagine having an open, honest conversation with someone important in your life. What would you share? How would you speak your truth?

Technique:
Create a journal where you write down your feelings and thoughts regularly. Allow yourself to speak openly and honestly, without fear of judgment. This practice will strengthen your ability to communicate openly in your relationships.

E – Expression, Esteem, Empowerment

Expression:

1. **How would my life change if I gave myself full permission to express myself honestly, even when it's uncomfortable?**
   What's the worst that could happen if you let yourself speak your truth — and the best?

2. **What creative outlets can I use to express emotions I've been holding inside?**
   Whether through writing, art, dance, or another form, what medium will help you release what you've been bottling up?

Technique:
Set aside a time each week for creative expression, without judgment. Whether it's painting, journaling, or singing, allow yourself to express freely and without expectations.

Esteem:

1. **What small victories can I celebrate today?**
   No matter how small, identify one thing you've done today that you can be proud of. How does acknowledging it change the way you see yourself?

2. **What would happen if I started to see myself as my biggest cheerleader?**
   Imagine being your own biggest fan. What does that look like in terms of actions, words, and beliefs?

Technique:
Start a "celebration jar" where you write down your wins and moments of self-appreciation. When you're feeling low, read them back to remind yourself of your strength and progress.

Empowerment:

1. **What decision can I make today that reflects my true values and beliefs?**
   Think about a choice you need to make. What would it

look like to make it from a place of power and authenticity?

2. **What would it mean to take full ownership of my life and my decisions?**
   What are you waiting for? What would happen if you stepped fully into the driver's seat of your own life?

Technique:
Each morning, set an intention for the day that aligns with your core values. Take one action — no matter how small — that brings you closer to living in alignment with your truth.

APPENDIX 2

Self-Assessment: Rate Your ACE Level

The following self-assessment is designed to help you track your progress as you move through the ACE framework. This tool will help you reflect on where you are in your journey, identify growth areas, and celebrate the strides you've made. The assessment is broken into three parts: Awareness, Care, and Expression — the key components of the ACE framework. As you answer each question, rate yourself on a scale of 1 to 5, where:

- **1 = Strongly Disagree** (This is an area I'm really struggling with.)
- **2 = Disagree** (I'm working on this but haven't fully embraced it yet.)
- **3 = Neutral** (I'm in between; I'm aware but haven't fully committed to change.)
- **4 = Agree** (I'm making progress in this area.)
- **5 = Strongly Agree** (I feel confident and consistent in this area.)

A – Awareness, Affection, Affirmation

Awareness

1. I am able to recognise the negative influences and beliefs that have shaped my self-perception.

2. I acknowledge how past experiences (trauma, relationships, etc.) have affected my confidence.
3. I regularly reflect on my emotional state and make time to evaluate my growth.

Affection

1. I show myself compassion and treat myself with kindness.
2. I have stopped being overly critical of myself and am learning to embrace self-love.
3. I can forgive myself for past mistakes without holding onto guilt.

Affirmation

1. I use positive affirmations to counteract negative self-talk.
2. I believe in my worth and speak positively to myself.
3. I affirm my strengths and capabilities every day.

C – Care, Connection, Communication

Care

1. I prioritise my physical, emotional, and mental well-being through regular self-care practices.
2. I engage in activities that replenish me and reduce stress.
3. I recognise the importance of rest and relaxation in maintaining my energy.

Connection

1. I seek out relationships that support and uplift me.
2. I've built a network of people who encourage my growth and success.
3. I feel understood and accepted in my personal and professional relationships.

Communication

1. I express my needs clearly and without guilt.
2. I set and enforce boundaries with ease and confidence.
3. I communicate openly about my emotions and desires, even when it's uncomfortable.

E – Expression, Esteem, Empowerment

Expression

1. I feel free to express my feelings and desires, without fear of judgment.
2. I regularly engage in creative activities (journaling, art, etc.) to express myself.
3. I share my authentic self with others and do not hide behind a mask.

Esteem

1. I recognise and celebrate my achievements, no matter how small.
2. I believe in my inherent value and worth, regardless of external circumstances.

3. I actively affirm my strengths and give myself credit for my progress.

Empowerment

1. I feel confident in making decisions that align with my values and beliefs.
2. I take consistent action toward my goals, trusting that I am capable of achieving them.
3. I have stepped into my power, and I make choices that reflect my authentic self.

Scoring Your ACE Level

After rating yourself on each statement, tally up your total score for each section (A, C, and E). The possible total score for each section is between 3 and 15. Add your total scores for each section to get your **overall ACE score.**

Total Score Breakdown:

- **45-50: Empowered & Confident**
  You are well on your way to reclaiming your full confidence. You are actively embracing the ACE framework and integrating it into your life. Your self-awareness, self-compassion, and empowerment are strong, and you are clearly on the path to sustained growth. Continue to build on these strengths, and keep celebrating your achievements. You're living from a place of authentic power!

- **35-44: Progressing & Growing**
  You're making meaningful strides in reclaiming your confidence. You've already begun to put the ACE

framework into practice, but there are still areas that require some attention and nurturing. Keep working on deepening your connection to yourself, setting clearer boundaries, and expressing your needs. You're moving forward, and that's something to celebrate.

- **25-34: Developing & Learning**
  You're in the process of rediscovering your confidence, and it's okay to be where you are. You have identified areas for growth, but you may still be uncertain or hesitant in some aspects of the ACE framework. This is a time of learning and refining. Focus on taking small, consistent actions that will help you build a stronger foundation. Be patient and compassionate with yourself.

- **15-24: Beginning & Reflecting**
  You're in the early stages of your journey to reclaiming your confidence. You may be struggling with self-doubt, fear, or limiting beliefs. This score indicates a need for deeper self-reflection and a commitment to embracing the ACE framework. Start by focusing on the basics: awareness of your thoughts and emotions, self-compassion, and allowing yourself to express your needs. Every step, no matter how small, is a step toward reclaiming your power.

Using Your Score to Guide Your Growth

Once you've calculated your score, take some time to reflect on the areas where you scored the lowest. What specific actions can you take to improve in those areas? The ACE framework is a journey, not a destination. Each score reflects where you are now, and with continued effort, you will see growth.

- **For low scores in Awareness:** Start by setting aside time each day for self-reflection. Journaling can be a powerful tool to help you identify patterns and beliefs that may be holding you back. Try using the open-ended questions from the previous section to guide your reflections.

- **For low scores in Care:** Prioritising your well-being is crucial for building confidence. Begin small by incorporating one self-care activity into your routine — whether it's taking a walk, meditating, or just resting. You don't have to do it all at once; small acts of care can yield big results.

- **For low scores in Expression:** Look for ways to express yourself more freely. Start by writing or talking about your feelings with someone you trust. Creative outlets like painting, dancing, or even singing can also help release emotions and strengthen your confidence.

Remember, **this assessment is a tool for growth**. It's meant to help you see where you are and where you're headed. Celebrate your progress, no matter how small, and continue to take steps toward reclaiming your confidence and stepping into your full power.

REFERENCES & NOTES

1. Brown, B. (2010). *The Gifts of Imperfection: Let Go of Who You Think You're Supposed to Be and Embrace Who You Are.* Hazelden Publishing.

    - Brené Brown's work on vulnerability, shame, and courage has been instrumental in understanding the role of vulnerability in building confidence and connection.

2. Neff, K. D. (2011). *Self-Compassion: The Proven Power of Being Kind to Yourself.* William Morrow Paperbacks.

    - Kristin Neff's exploration of self-compassion provided me with the tools to embrace self-care and show affection to myself without guilt.

3. Germer, C. K., & Neff, K. D. (2013). *The Mindful Self-Compassion Workbook: A Proven Way to Accept Yourself, Build Inner Strength, and Thrive.* The Guilford Press.

    - This resource guided me through the transformative process of practicing self-compassion, a key aspect of reclaiming confidence.

4. Tolle, E. (2004). *The Power of Now: A Guide to Spiritual Enlightenment.* New World Library.

    - Eckhart Tolle's insights on being present and reconnecting with the inner self have been essential in my understanding of **awareness** and **self-empowerment**.

5. Goleman, D. (1995). *Emotional Intelligence: Why It Can Matter More Than IQ*. Bantam Books.
   - Daniel Goleman's work on emotional intelligence helped me understand how emotional awareness and control are integral to confidence building and healthy communication.

Journal Articles:

1. Kegan, R., & Lahey, L. L. (2009). *Immunity to Change: How to Overcome It and Unlock the Potential in Yourself and Your Organization*. Harvard Business Review.
   - This article expanded my understanding of how individuals can overcome internal barriers to change and personal growth, relevant to the process of reclaiming confidence.

2. Dweck, C. S. (2006). *Mindset: The New Psychology of Success*. Random House.
   - Carol Dweck's research on "fixed" and "growth" mindsets was pivotal in understanding how our beliefs about our own abilities shape our confidence and success.

3. Wallerstein, J. S. (1996). *The Psychological Effects of Divorce on Children. Family and Conciliation Courts Review*, 34(2), 177-196.
   - This article provided valuable insights into the emotional effects of major life transitions, particularly divorce, and how they impact confidence and self-esteem.

Websites & Online Resources:

1. The Center for Compassion and Altruism Research and Education (CCARE). (n.d.). *What is Compassion?*. Retrieved from https://ccare.stanford.edu

    o CCARE's research on compassion and its connection to self-care and emotional well-being informed my approach to the **Affection** component of the ACE framework.

2. Psychology Today. (2019). *Building Self-Esteem: What Works and What Doesn't*. Retrieved from https://www.psychologytoday.com

    o The articles on self-esteem and confidence in Psychology Today helped me understand the practical tools for building self-worth, which are central to the **Esteem** step.

3. Mindful.org. (2017). *How Mindfulness Can Help You Overcome Self-Doubt*. Retrieved from https://www.mindful.org

    o Mindful.org's articles on mindfulness and its role in overcoming negative thought patterns supported the research behind the **Awareness** step of the ACE framework.

The Bible:

1. Please note that bible references in this book have been taken from the following versions: New International Version (NIV), New Living Translation (NLT) and King James Version (KJV)

Podcasts & Interviews:

1. Oprah's Super Soul Conversations. (2019). *Brené Brown on Vulnerability, Courage, and the Power of Self-Worth.*
   - Brené Brown's insights on vulnerability and courage have been a foundational influence on understanding the link between **vulnerability** and confidence.

2. The School of Greatness Podcast. (2020). *Lewis Howes: The Power of Self-Love and Healing Trauma.*
   - Lewis Howes' interviews with thought leaders helped shape my understanding of how self-love and healing can restore confidence and personal power.

Miscellaneous Resources:

1. *The Self-Esteem Workbook* by Glenn R. Schiraldi (2006). New Harbinger Publications.
   - This workbook provided exercises and practices that were integral to strengthening my own self-esteem and led to the development of the **Esteem** section of the ACE framework.

2. *Radical Acceptance: Embracing Your Life With the Heart of a Buddha* by Tara Brach (2003). Bantam.
   - Tara Brach's teachings on radical acceptance offered a profound perspective on self-compassion and the importance of embracing our flaws as a pathway to confidence.

OTHER BOOKS BY THE AUTHOR

FLOW: Living From Drought To Abundance

Finding Self in A Loveless Marriage

Extraordinary Living: 365 Days of Inspiration

OPEN TO LOVE: A Modern Woman's Memoir on Being Single and Happy

HIS LADY: 5 Traits of a Godly Ambitious Woman

THE PURPOSE-DRIVEN CAREER: 3 Breakthrough Steps to Find Happiness, Joy, and Fulfilment in Your Career

ABOUT THE AUTHOR

Aji R. Michael is a master coach, life stylist, and bestselling author whose transformative books have empowered countless individuals to lead lives of health, elegance, and fulfilment. With over a decade of experience in the fast-paced health and care sector, Aji has become a beacon of guidance for professionals seeking growth, balance, and purpose.

Inspired by her deep passion for transforming lives, Aji founded *Redefining Living*, a social enterprise dedicated to empowering individuals to live well, feel well, and age well in the comfort of their homes. Through *His Lady*, Aji further extends her mission to empower women. *His Lady* (www.hislady.org) helps women rebuild their lives on the foundation of faith, renew their souls through self-care and spiritual growth, and rise to their true purpose with confidence and grace. With programs, community, and resources designed to inspire, Aji guides women toward a life of abundance aligned with God's will.

Aji's work through her books, podcasts, videos, and businesses reflects her dedication to inspiring others to live meaningful lives anchored in faith, grace, and love.

AKNOWLEDGEMENTS

There's a special bond that forms when kindred spirits meet — a bond that brings about deep healing and transformation. Often, it feels as though God has strategically placed us in each other's lives at just the right moment to facilitate the healing we both need. I have been blessed to experience this profound connection with many incredible women, and I am truly grateful for that.

To the women who shared your stories with me, **thank you**. Your transparency, courage, and openness have healed me and affirmed my calling. Your willingness to be vulnerable and share your journey has enriched this book in ways I can never fully express. I am deeply moved by the trust you've shown me, and I carry that with me in every word written here.

To my sisters in the **His Lady group**, thank you for your openness and support. Your insights, your courage, and your stories have inspired this writing in ways that words can hardly capture. Each of you has contributed to this book's heart and purpose, and I am forever grateful for the space you've allowed me to hold with you.

To my soul sister, **Feyikemi Oyewole**, words can't fully convey my gratitude. Thank you for being a source of power and vulnerability, for holding space for me even during moments when I doubted myself. Your unwavering belief in me, even when I couldn't see it for myself, has been a light in my life. Thank you for your critical review of this book — your guidance has made this work stronger, sharper, and more impactful. I am so blessed to have you by my side.

To all of you, my dear sisters, thank you for walking this journey with me. This book is as much yours as it is mine.

www.ingramcontent.com/pod-product-compliance
Lightning Source LLC
Chambersburg PA
CBHW030042100526
44590CB00011B/302